La...

WESTERN
CRETE

a countryside guide
Ninth edition

Jonnie Godfrey
and
Elizabeth Karslake

SUNFLOWER BOOKS

Ninth edition © 2017
Sunflower Books™
PO Box 36160
London SW7 3WS, UK
www.sunflowerbooks.co.uk

ISBN 978-1-85691-490-1

Church at Stalos (Walk 1)

Important note to the reader ⎯⎯⎯⎯

We have done our best to ensure that the descriptions and maps in this book are error-free at press date. The book will be updated, where necessary, whenever future printings permit. It will be very helpful for us to receive your comments (sent in care of the publishers, please) for the updating of future printings.

We also rely on those who use this book — especially walkers — to take along a good supply of common sense when they explore. Conditions change fairly rapidly on Crete, and *storm damage or bulldozing may make a route unsafe at any time*. If the route is not as we outline it here, and your way ahead is not secure, return to the point of departure. ***Never attempt to complete a tour or walk under hazardous conditions!*** Please read carefully the notes on pages 37 to 44, as well as the introductory comments at the beginning of each tour and walk (regarding road conditions, equipment, grade, distances and time, etc). Explore *safely*, while at the same time respecting the beauty of the countryside.

Cover photograph: Samaria Gorge

Photographs: Elizabeth Karslake, with the exception of pages 70 (Jonnie Godfrey); 120, 131 (Tanya Tsikas); 127 (Footscapes of Crete); 13, 15, 18-9, 22-3, 30-1, 32 (right), 34, 42, 54, 60-1 (both), 65, 66-7, 113 (right), 124 and cover (Shutterstock)
Maps: Nick Hill for Sunflower Books. Base map data © OpenStreetMap contributors. Contour data made available under ODbL (opendata commons.org/licenses/odbl/1.0)
A CIP catalogue record for this book is available from the British Library.
Printed and bound in England: Short Run Press, Exeter

Contents

4 Landscapes of Western Crete

View east towards the Ida Mountains (Psiloritis), from near Melindaou (Walk 20)

Preface

Mountains rearing straight up from the sea, deep wooded gorges, ravines and valleys — and yet more glorious mountains, standing proud and acting as a magnet to the eye and the imagination — that's Western Crete, or real Crete, as some would say. Its strong, dramatic scenery and colours create sweeping landscapes of harsh but beautiful countryside — countryside that has been the backdrop for heroic deeds, ancient civilisations and constant intrigue for thousands of years, and the home of obdurate, tough-spirited people — made so by their labours on the land and their experiences.

Getting to know Western Crete takes time; the number of people who explore beyond the obvious is slowly growing. We hope we will lead you straight to the heart of the matter with this book, whether you are a first- or second-time visitor unsure about how best to get to know the island or, indeed, if you are someone who doesn't need convincing but would like a reliable, thorough and different guide. We encourage you to explore to the full. We won't need to inspire you; one look at Western Crete will do that.

Landscapes of Western Crete, in the same tried and tested format as the other titles in the series, takes you well off the beaten track, while at the same time describing in full the most popular touring routes and excursions. This Ninth edition is a thorough update.

Everyone has heard of the Samaria Gorge, and rightly so. But frankly, anyone who contemplates walking the gorge — a long and by no means unchallenging expedition — could accomplish a number of other walks in this book and gain a great amount of pleasure in alternative landscapes. What's more, walking almost anywhere else in Western Crete will give the added bonus of solitude and perhaps an even greater feeling for the island and its people, who vary both in style and character from region to region.

Acknowledging the fact that Western Crete attracts a number of visitors who choose to have more than one base, or who don't feel obliged to return to their villa, hotel or apartment every night, we have described walks that can be linked and which cover a large expanse of the

5

Elizabeth (left) and Jonnie

western end of the island. Western Crete lends itself to this arrangement very well. These walks start on the shoulders of the awe-inspiring White Mountains *(Levka Ori)* — even when they're not snow-capped, their peaks are a striking white, hence their name — and descend to the south coast, from where you can head either west or east.

We have been asked, often, if and how western and eastern Crete differ from one another. In fact we naturally made the comparison ourselves in the course of compiling this guide, having previously written *Landscapes of Eastern Crete*. The west is even more mountainous and has developed more slowly than the east; the geography is such that walks tend to be longer and the terrain, on the whole, rougher in the west. And the people of Western Crete are somewhat more reserved than their counterparts in the east. Western Crete has its own captivating and entrancing character. You simply need to immerse yourself in the countryside to find out.

— JONNIE GODFREY

Acknowledgements

Many thanks to all the users who send us helpful updates, to the friends who initially hiked with us, to Liz and Paul Marsden of Footscapes of Crete for help with the Seventh edition, and to Mike Hyde who followed in our footsteps with his GPS and logged the original GPS tracks for this guide.

Background reading

John Bowman: *The Travellers' Guide: Crete*
Pat Cameron: *Blue Guide Crete*
David MacNeil Doren: *The Winds of Crete* (John Murray)
Adam Hopkins: *Crete: Past, Present & Peoples* (Faber)
Nikos Kazantzakis: *Zorba the Greek* (Faber)
Patrick Leigh Fermor: *Abducting a General* (John Murray)
W Stanley Moss: *Ill Met by Moonlight* (Buchan and Enwright)
Oleg Polunin: *Flowers of the Mediterranean* (Chatto)
Oliver Rackham and Jennifer Moody: *The Making of the Cretan Landscape* (Manchester University Press)

Getting about

Hiring a car is certainly one of the best ways to get to know Crete. We hope that by giving you some good itineraries, you will be able to make the most of the island — and your car. Many of the tours we suggest will take you past the starting- and/or end-points of several walks. In fact, seeing the countryside from a car will encourage you, we hope, to go off the beaten track and into the hills with us, on foot.

Taxis are an alternative way to tour and, if shared, can be a reasonably-priced way to travel. Do agree a fare before setting out, if it's going to be an unmetered trip. If necessary, your holiday company's agent or representative will help you to find a driver who speaks English and who will be happy and proud to show off his island.

Organised excursions are good value; coaches eat up the kilometres while you sit back and watch it all go by.

One of the best ways of getting about is by **local bus**. Once you've done it for the first time, you'll realise it's economical, reliable and entertaining. You'll whizz along the highways and bumble through villages with a bus-eye view over the countryside. Use the local bus network to explore Western Crete economically. The plans overleaf locate the bus stations in Hania and Rethimnon. Timetables for buses covering the western half of the island are on pages 133-134. *Note: Even if you have downloaded timetables from the web (see page 133), do pick up a current bus timetable* at the station before you plan any excursions: the frequency of services changes with the seasons. For complete assurance, verify the times in advance by asking. If you are lucky, the officials at Hania bus station (where, incidentally, there is a left luggage facility) will tell you the number of the bus you want; arrive in good time, as buses leave promptly and sometimes even *earlier* than scheduled, particularly those that depart at the crack of dawn. Most tickets are bought at the depot before boarding, including those to Samaria (the 'Omalos' bus). If you *do* buy tickets on the bus, don't be confused if you get three per person for just one trip — they add up to the total. You can flag down buses en route, but they don't always stop. *Always* put your hand out, even at a bus stop.

HANIA — KEY

1   Tourist information bureau
2   Tourist police
3   Greek Alpine Club (EOS)
4   Post office
5   Telephone and telegraph (OTE)
6   National Bank of Greece
7   Bank of Greece
8   🚌 for Akrotiri
9   🚌 for Akrotiri, Iraklion, Souda, Mournies and town routes
10 🚌 for Alikianos, Aptera (beach), Hora Sfakion, Kalamaki,
     Kandanos, Kastelli-Kissamos, Lakki, Meskla, Omalos (Samaria),
     Paleohora, Platanias (beach), Platanos, Rethimnon, Sougia,
     Xiloskala (Samaria)
11 Stadium
12 Ionian and Popular Bank
13 Public gardens and zoo
14 Market
15 Shivao bastion
16 Venetian loggia
17 Archaeological museum
18 Maritime museum (Firka tower)
19 Customs
20 Cathedral
21 Minaret
22 Hospital
23 Venetian lighthouse
24 Synagogue

RETHIMNON — KEY

1. Tourist information bureau (on Venizelou, about 300m/yds east of Platia Iroon)
2. Post office
3. 🚌 Bus station
4. Public beach
5. Youth hostel
6. Greek Commercial Bank
7. National Bank of Greece
8. Arimondi fountain
9. Nerantzes fountain
10. Venetian fortress
11. Venetian harbour
12. Museum (Venetian loggia)
13. Public gardens
14. Bank of Greece
15. Stadium
16. 🚕 Taxi rank
17. Telephone and telegraph (OTE)
18. Town hall
19. Archaeological museum
20. Lighthouse
21. Hospital

🌻 Picnicking

Picnicking on Crete is not an organised affair. There are very few specially-provided sites; it's very much a case of pick your own olive tree and toss for the best view. Following is a selection of some good places to throw down a towel or a rug (it's unlikely to be wet, but it might well be prickly) and revel in the countryside. Don't forget the corkscrew ...

These picnic suggestions have been chosen for ease of access, and none involves too much climbing or lugging of provisions. We tell you how to get there (including waypoints so that you can set your satnav if you like) and how long a walk you'll have. Naturally, all these picnic strolls can be extended to make satisfying short walks.

Note that *picnic numbers correspond to walk numbers:* on the corresponding *walking* map the precise location of the picnic spot is shown on by the symbol *P*. (The three suggestions prefixed 'CT' are specifically linked to the corresponding car tours.)

All picnickers should read the Country code on page 13 and go quietly in the countryside.

1 Agia Lake *(map page 47; photographs pages 13 and 22)*
allow 5-30min on foot
🚗 Following Car tour 3, from **Agia** drive towards 'KIRTO-MADOS' and park on the track to the lake, just beyond a bridge with iron railings (35° 28.632'N, 23° 55.788'E). Now it's only 5min to a pleasant spot by the lake. For a longer walk, park on the main road in **Agia** (35° 28.346'N, 23° 55.854'E) and follow the Short walk on page 45.

These pleasant hillsides below Polirinia are the setting for Picnic 13.

2 Kotsifou Gorge *(map page 49, photograph page 32)*
allow about 40min on foot
🚗 Following Car tour 3, park in **Plakias** (35° 11.423'N, 24° 23.714'E). Follow Short walk 2 on page 48 to the GORGE and MILL.

3 Diktamos Gorge *(map pages 50-51, photograph page 51)*
allow 5-15min on foot
🚗 Follow Car tour 5. Coming downhill into **Katohori**, on a big U-bend to the right (by a miniature concrete church), take the road to the left. Continue 400m to a small square and park (35° 26.285'N, 24° 3.947'E).Then follow Walk 3, page 50 and either picnic at the small PICNIC SITE (under 5min) or in the GORGE itself (from about 15min).

4 Kambi *(map page 55)*
allow 10-30min on foot
🚗 Follow Car tour 5 and park in **Kambi** near the church (35° 25.078'N, 24° 4.178'E). Then follow Walk 4 (page 52) as far as PICNIC AREA below right.

6 Kournas Lake *(map page 59, photographs pages 60-61)*
allow about 10min on foot
🚗 Follow Car tour 6 on page 32. Having passed the lake at **Kournas**, park near the bridge (35° 20.304'N, 24° 16.695'E). Then either just find a nice spot or use the map and notes for Walk 6 to stretch your legs.

8 Rethimnon *(map page 69)*
allow up to 5min on foot
🚗 Car tours 6, 7, and 8 take you to **Rethimnon**. From the town drive up to the chapel of **Profitis Ilias**. To get there, head south uphill on Theotokopoulou Street (at the eastern side of the town; this is the road to ROUSSOSPITI). Turn right on the track to the CHURCH and park (35° 21.417'N, 24° 29.036'E). Picnic here, or in the PINES five minutes above the chapel (see notes for Walk 8 on page 66).

9 Myli Gorge *(map page 69, photographs on pages 68 and 70)*
allow about 10min on foot
🚗 Car tours 6, 7, and 8 take you to **Rethimnon**. From there **Myli** and its gorge can be reached as a detour either via Roussospiti or via Perivolia (see the map on page 69; 35° 20.258'N, 24° 30.236'E). Follow Walk 9 on page 70 for as long as you like.

13 Polirinia *(map page 79, photograph opposite)*
allow 20-25min on foot
🚗 Follow Car tour 1 and take the DETOUR TO **Polirinia**. Park near the taverna at the end of the road (35° 27.305'N, 23° 39.040'E) and use the map to walk south out of the village. Picnic just past the last houses.

14 Katsomatados *(map page 82, photograph page 83)*
allow under 10min on foot
🚗 Follow Car tour 1 to **Katsomatados**, 3km south of Topolia (35° 24.328'N, 23° 40.933'E). Then use notes on page 80 to picnic near the start of Walk 14.

17 Sougia *(map pages 88-89, photographs page 89)*
allow about 10-15min on foot
🚗 Following Car tour 3, park in **Sougia** (35° 14.828'N, 23° 48.423'E). Use the notes for Walk 17 on page 88 to picnic in the GORGE.

25 Imbros Gorge *(map page 113, photograph page 113, left)*
allow about 20min on foot
🚗 Follow Car tour 6 to the

Picnic CT8 is set at this delightful old bridge over the Platys River in the Amari Valley.

ENTRANCE TO THE GORGE and park (35° 15.231'N, 24° 10.281'E). Then use notes on page 112 to picnic along the route of Walk 25. If you go far enough into the gorge, you may have to pay.

27 Megalopotamos River
(map page 119)
allow under 5min on foot
🚗 Follow Car tour 6 past **Asomatos**, to the arched BRIDGE over the Megalopotamos River (35° 10.441'N, 24° 27.958'E).

28 Kaloidena Chapel
(map page 124)
allow 5min to 20min on foot
🚗 Follow Car tour 8 to **Ano Meros** and park (35° 11.237'N, 24° 39.659'E). Then follow the first 20min of Walk 28 (page 122) to the pretty chapel with its spring and picnic area. *Hint:* you *could* even drive there: follow the road from Ano Meros towards HORDAKI, then turn right uphill at the brown signpost 'KALOIDENA MONASTERY'.

31 Eleftherna *(map page 132, photo page 131)*
allow under 10min to 1h on foot
🚗 Drive from Rethimnon (Car tours 6, 7, 8) to **Archaia**

Eleftherna (35° 19.416'N, 24° 40.590'E). Follow Walk 31 (page 130) to picnic at the BYZANTINE TOWER — or go as far as you like (the HELLENISTIC BRIDGE reached in 1h is a particularly pleasant setting).

CT4 Moni Gouverneto *(touring map and map page 71)*
allow 5-10min on foot
🚗 Follow Car tour 4 to **Moni Gouverneto** (35° 35.075'N, 24° 8.406'E). There are good places on the hillside below the monastery, but little shade.

CT6 Kourtaliotiko Gorge
(touring map and map page 119)
5min down on foot, 10min up
🚗 Follow Car tour 6 from **Asomatos** (page 31); park 600m along the gorge (35° 11.659'N, 24° 27.830'E), to picnic at the **Agios Nikolaos** chapel.

CT8 Amari Valley *(touring map, photograph above)*
allow under 5min on foot
🚗 From the south side of the bridge over the **Platys River** (125.5km on Car tour 8, page 36) take the slip road down to the BRIDGE shown above to picnic (35° 10.371'N, 24° 41.708'E).

For Picnic 1 you can either find a quiet corner of the lake at Agia or sit by this attractive modern bridge

Country code for walkers and motorists

Observance of certain unwritten rules is essential when out walking or driving in the countryside anywhere, but particularly on Crete's rugged terrain, where irresponsible behaviour can lead to dangerous mistakes. Whether you are an experienced rambler or not, it is important to adhere to a country code, to avoid causing damage, harming animals, or even endangering your own life.

— **Do not light fires**; everything gets tinder dry.
— **Do not frighten animals.** The goats and sheep you may encounter are not used to strangers. By making a noise, trying to touch or photograph them, you may cause them to run in fear and be hurt.
— **Walk quietly** through all farms, hamlets and villages, and leave all gates just as you found them, wherever they are. Although animals may not be in evidence, the gates *do* have a purpose.
— **Protect all wild and cultivated plants.** Don't pick fruit if it looks like it is somebody else's livelihood. You'll doubtless be offered some en route, anyhow. Avoid walking over cultivated land.
— **Take all your litter** away.

— When **driving**, never block roads or tracks. Park where you will not inconvenience anyone or cause danger.

And especially for walkers:
— **Do not take risks.** Do not attempt walks beyond your capacity and do not wander off the paths described if there is any sign of gathering mist or if it is late in the day.
— **Do not walk alone** and *always* tell a responsible person *exactly* where you are going and when you plan to return. On any but a very short walk near villages, take a mobile, GPS or compass, whistle, torch, extra water and warm clothing, as well as some high energy food, like chocolate. Although this may sound 'over the top' to an inexperienced walker, it could save your life.

13

Touring

Crete is a very large island, and most visitors hire a car for some part of their stay to try to get to grips with it.

It pays to hire for a minimum of three days and, while you may find cheaper rates with smaller firms, remember that the larger companies offer the advantage of representation all over the island. Since it's likely that you'll want to cover a lot of ground, you'll be in a better position with a well-known company should anything go wrong.

We recommend the **1:100,000 maps 'Central Crete'** and **'Western Crete'** published by Terrain Cartography for touring, but *beware:* their 'smooth dirt road' is, in our experience, only suitable for 4WD! Remember that your car hire contact will no doubt prohibit off-road driving and that **tyres** are *not* covered by insurance; you won't be charged for a simple puncture, but ruined tyres will have to be paid for! Be sure you understand the terms of the hire contract. Keep your hire contract, passport and driving licence with you at all times when out on the road. Take note of the hire company's telephone numbers (both office hours and *out of hours*), just in case. **Petrol** is widely available, but it is still a good idea to set out with plenty.

Our car touring notes are brief; they include little information readily available in standard guidebooks or the handouts you can obtain free from tourist offices and tourist information kiosks at home or on Crete. Instead, we've concentrated on the 'logistics' of touring: times and distances, road conditions, and giving clear directions where you might falter or be misled — for instance, by lack of signposting. Most of all, we emphasise possibilities for **walking** and **picnicking**. While some of the suggestions for short walks and picnics may not be suitable during a long car tour, you may find a landscape that you would like to explore at leisure another day. (Note that references in brackets at the top of a tour refer to walks and picnics that can be easily reached by *detouring* off the main route.)

Our pull-out touring maps are ideal for planning and in fact contain all the information you will need outside the towns. The tours have been written up with Hania as departure/return point, but can quite easily be joined from other centres. Plans of Hania and Rethimnon are on pages 8-9.

SOME POINTS WORTH NOTING

We cannot stress too strongly the advantage of taking with you a good guide to Crete's history and archaeological heritage; see page 6. Note also:

— **Allow plenty of time for visits**; the times we give for the tours include only very brief stops at viewpoints labelled (☎) in the notes.

— **Telephones**, with meters, are located at most kiosks, at OTE (telephone exchanges) and in *cafeneions*. Many telephone boxes are card phones; buy cards at kiosks.

— WC indicates **public toilets**; these are rare, but others are found in restaurants.

— Don't be flummoxed by **Greek road signs**; they are almost invariably followed by English ones.

— You are meant to cross a **solid white line near the edge of the road**, when someone wants to overtake. However, beware of slower vehicles, laden donkeys, bikes, etc ahead, when you round corners.

— Conversely, **a solid white line in the middle of the road** means NO OVER-TAKING — regardless of the behaviour of motorists who appear not to notice it.

— **Do think** before you pull up to admire a view, if you are not at a viewpoint with parking; remember that other motorists cannot see round corners.

— Never throw **cigarette ends** out of the car.

— Come to a standstill at **stop signs**.

— The spelling of **village names** may vary. We have used the letter 'H' where an 'X' or 'CH' might be used locally; this is to aid pronunciation.

— In towns, only **park** your car where permitted.

— **Priority signs** (red/black/white arrows) on narrow stretches of road give priority to the *black* arrow.

— You will see many **shrines** beside the road (they vary from little boxes topped by a cross and filled with oil, a candle, icon or pictures to very elaborate miniature churches like the one shown above). They warn travellers that sometime in the past a fatal or near-fatal accident involving motor vehicles has occurred at that spot. **Drive carefully!**

Distances quoted are *cumulative kilometres* from Hania. A key to the symbols in the notes is on the touring map. Do note, however, that only the largest churches — or churches that are landmarks — have been highlighted, since every village has at least one church. The same can be said of tavernas or *cafeneions;* food and drink can be found almost anywhere.

All motorists should read the Country code on page 13 and go quietly in the countryside. *Kalo taxithee!*

Car tour 1: THE FAR WEST

Hania • (Kastelli-Kissamos) • (Polirinia) • Vathi • Moni Chriso-skalitisas • (Elafonisi) • Elos • Topolia • Hania

164km/102mi; about 5 hours'
driving; Exit B from Hania (town
plan page 8). We use the old north
coast road to begin, not the A90
highway. All roads are quite good.

Walks en route: 1, (11), (12),
(13), 14, 15, (18)
Picnic suggestions (see pages
10-13): (13 at Polirinia), 14 at
Katsomatados

Y ou can drive miles through this wild, rugged western
end of Crete and see virtually no-one; on this tour,
you're alone in the landscape, once you leave the north
coast. The sea views are dramatic on the coastal drive and
contrast well with the countryside inland on the return
journey. Try to set off early in the morning, so you have
time for a detour to the turquoise shallows at Elafonisi.

From 1866 Square, take Exit B
(Skalidi, then Kissamou). There
will be plenty of petrol stations
along the north coast road, so
fill up (⛽) before turning off.
Very shortly past the turning left
to Theriso (1.2km) you come to
a large Y-fork: be sure to go
right here for 'PLATANIAS',
leaving the route to Omalos and
the A90 national highway off to
the left. Continue west on the
old north coast road. All the
beach-side villages on this route
— **Galatas, Kalamaki, Glaros,
Kato Stalos** (where Walk 1
begins and ends), **Agia Marina**
(△), **Platanias** — have tavernas
and rooms and apartments for
rent (▲▲▲△✕).
Cross the Keritis River (12km)
and drive on (⛽ 13.6km),
flanked by orange groves and
large patches of bamboo (⛽
15.5km). Soon the route passes
through **Maleme** (16km
▲▲✕⛽). The village saw violent
activity during the Second
World War; it was here that the
Battle of Crete flared up. At
17km you pass the Hotel Mikes
on the right; the first turning left
past the hotel, signposted to
Vlacheronista, leads to the

German War Graves (also
signposted, in German and
Greek.
Continue along the north coast,
hemming the sea. You will see
the Rodopou Peninsula (Walks
11 and 12) lunging out ahead in
the middle distance. Drive
through **Tavronitis** (19.5km
✕⛽). **Kamisiana** (20.5km ✕)
and **Rapaniana** (21km ✝▲▲
✕⛽) flash by. On your way
through **Skoutelonas** (22km),
look to the right, at the
beginning of the peninsula, to
see Moni Gonia (Walk 12).
There is a wide three-way
junction of roads at **Kolimbari**
(where Walk 12 begins and
ends). A turning right (signed to
Afrata) goes into Kolimbari and
to the Gonia Monastery — see
them at leisure another day, or
plan to do Walk 12. Go sharp
left at this junction, towards
'KISSAMOS', joining the A90
national highway after 1km,
again heading west towards
'KISSAMOS'. After less than 4km
you could turn off right for
'BEACH OF RAVDOUCHA' and
then follow signs for 'RODOPOU'
to get to Walk 11.
The main tour keeps to the A90.

16

Soon, on the outskirts of Kissamos, the Gramvousa Peninsula is visible. The national highway passes through the centre of **Kastelli-Kissamos★** (**⛺🏔️✕🚻M**). The town is certainly worth visiting; it has a pleasant atmosphere. But we suggest you come another day, when you will have time to combine a visit with a walk or a swim at Falasarna's beach.

(*Detour:* As you drive through Kissamos, watch for a turn-off left to Polirinia at a junction with a central triangle, opposite a petrol station (37.5km 🚻). If and when you take this detour, you'll first pass a new church on the left and then continue inland, passing another sign for Polirinia at 39km. Go through Karfiana and Grigoriana before coming to Polirinia★ (44km

A good track extends almost to the end of the Gramvousa Peninsula, where bleached white sand fringes a mesmerising turquoise lagoon.

⚓✕). Drive to the end of the road and park near the taverna. Walk 13 ends here; if you'd like to stretch your legs, you could follow some of the walk in reverse, to the pleasant spot for Picnic 13 shown on page 10.)

Beyond the Polirinia turn-off you pass a small harbour and then the Kissamos port (41km). The Gramvousa Peninsula spreads before you directly to the right, a brown-grey mound disappearing into the sea. At 47.5km a road (rough for the last kilometre) leads down right to Falasarna★ (⚓), where there is a good sandy beach — if you feel you have time for a swim. However, it will make your day very long to detour at this stage. If you decide to go for a swim, take the Elafonisi detour later in the day.

So keep up on the main road through **Platanos**, a long strung-out village. There's a good view back over the beach at 51km (📷); you can also see the tip of Falasarna. Then pass another good viewpoint at 53km (📷), over the Bay of

Moni Chrisoskalitisas (left) and Elafonisi (below)

Sfinari. In **Sfinari** (58km �ె) we turn away from the sea and head up into the hills. The road passes through the tiny hamlet of **Ano Sfinari** (60km) and winds along beside a ravine, rounding its end at 62km. Between **Kambos** (66km) and **Keramoti**, a village that juts out off the hillside, there is a steepish drop down to the sea. The village of **Amigdalokefali** is set mostly below the road, and then you pass through **Simadi** (77km), **Papadiana** (79km) and **Kefali** (81km ✕).

Half a kilometre beyond Kefali, turn right on a road that descends through tree-covered hillsides to **Vathi** (83km). Keep right at Vathi on the road to Chrisoskalitisas. Go through **Plokamiana** and by 90km you can at last see the monastery ahead with its bright blue roof. Turn left round the Bay of Stomio.

An ugly rash of houses has sprung up at **Chrisoskalitisas** (91km ✕), just before the monastery★ itself (92km ✝). Having visited the church, you're ready to start the return journey. But first, if you fancy a break and a swim, take the route going off right 0.5km past the monastery, signposted to Elafonisi. It leads to a lovely sandy beach and turquoise water — protected and created by the nearby Elafonisi Islands. Walk 18 can end at Elafonisi or the monastery.

Retracing the route from Chrisoskalitisas, turn right at 103.5km for 'HANIA'. Past **Louhi** (106km) fork right for 'ELOS'. **Elos** (108km ✕🍴) is a pretty village strung out through chestnut trees. Keep straight on at **Mili** (112km) and look out for any traffic coming in from the right (from Paleohora). Leave **Katsomatados** (Picnic 14; Walks 14 and 15) off to the right at 115.5km. Soon you will have a wonderful view through the Topolia Gorge★ (116.5km 📷). Just past this obvious viewpoint, there is a sign at the left of the road indicating the cave chapel of Agia Sophia★ (∩✝) up on the hillside. Go through the narrow tunnel in the gorge wall, then continue through the pretty hillside village of **Topolia** (118.5km), where Walk 15 ends, and **Voulgaro** (121.5km 🍴), where Walk 14 ends.

Reaching the old coast road at **Kaloudiana** (126km ✝), turn right for 'HANIA'. At **Koleni** (129km) turn left for 'NATIONAL ROAD'. Joining the A90 highway after 1km, make your way back to **Hania** (164km).

Car tour 2: PALEOHORA AND SOUTH COAST BEACHES

Hania • Tavronitis • Voukolies • Kandanos • Paleohora •
Kandanos • (Sougia) • Hania

152km/94mi; 4 hours' driving;
Exit B from Hania (town plan
page 8). Roads are good, but those
between Kandanos and Vlithias
are very narrow and winding.

Walks en route: 1, 17, (18)
Picnic suggestions (see pages
10-13): (17 at Sougia)

You will see two coasts on this trip — the north coast,
which you follow out of Hania, and the south coast
at Paleohora, where there is a long beach stretching for
miles east and west. The route cuts straight across the
island from north to south as far as Kandanos, before
descending torturously through Selinos (you will need a
good map!) as you search out the district's many frescoed
Byzantine churches. You might also like to make a detour
to Anidri, where there is a church of particular interest.

Follow Car tour 1 as far as
Tavronitis (19.5km). Here take
the left turn signposted
'NATIONAL ROAD, VOUKOLIES,
PALEOHORA'. Pass through
Neranztia (23.5km; ☕ at
25.5km) and, in **Voukolies**
(26km), go through the main
square. Then the main road
heads right uphill, climbing out
of this large village and the
valley. Wind up through olive
trees into the high hills. By
about 33km you can see over
the sea to the west coast on your
right. Then, at **Dromonero**
(34km), the countryside opens
out, and you enjoy some very
fine views. Driving through the
spread-out village of **Kako-
petros** (38km), follow the road
curving round to the right,
towards 'PALEOHORA'. Catch
your last glimpse of the north
coast — with the Gramvousa
Peninsula, shown on page 17,
jutting out into the sea. The
rockier landscape here is somewhat softened by horse chestnut
trees. **Mesavlia** (43.5km) is just
a few houses, followed by **Floria**
(47km) and **Anavanos**. At the
end of the village of **Kandanos**
(56km ☩☕), follow the road
round to the right. It then
makes a wide arc to the left and
heads south.

At **Plemeniana** (58km ☩) be

sure to see Agios Georgios church with its 15th-century frescoes. Some 2.5km further on, just past a cement works on the right, turn off right for ΦΑΚΟΣ (Sfakos; only signed in Greek at time of writing). Go through Sfakos and 0.5km further on, turn left (not signed) at a T-junction to **Kakodiki** (63km ♀) to see the church of St Isidore and the frescoed chapel of Mikhail Arkhangelos (♀). Then continue south, go through **Vlithias** (67km) and rejoin the main road. Soon the sea and the south coast come into view. Pass through **Kalamos** and **Ligia**, and then a rocky valley.

Paleohora (73.5km ⌂▲△✗🍴) is approached along an avenue of eucalyptus trees. Just 0.5km further on, you pass the turn-off for Anidri★, but it was not signposted at time of writing. If you would like to see the 14th-century frescoes in Anidri's Agios Georgios church (♀), just left just past the town hall (with flags), at handwritten signs for 'PALEOHORA CAMPING'. Then take the second left and carry straight on.

The main tour passes the Anidri turn-off and comes into Paleohora. Turn left just before the road narrows; you can see the clock tower ahead. Park on the sea-side esplanade. Walk 17, from Sougia via the site at Lisos, ends here, and Walk 18 to Elafonisi begins a taxi ride from here.

The simplest way to return to Hania is to retrace your outgoing route. But if you have decided to cover a lot of ground, it's possible to include Sougia in today's tour (add an extra hour). If you have a 4WD vehicle and can easily bump along unsurfaced roads, take the route via Anidri and Prodomi. Otherwise, drive northeast to Azogires and go via Strati and Temenia to Maza. From there follow the road through a gorge (🚶) down towards the sea. When you meet the main Hania/Sougia road, go right and start heading downhill to the coast. There's a good view of the towering wall of the White Mountains ahead of you as you descend. Drive through Moni and on to Sougia. To return from Sougia, pick up Car tour 3 at the 67km-point (page 23).

The harbour at Hania

Car tour 3: COUNTRYSIDE, COASTAL BACKWATER AND HIGH CRETAN PASTURELAND

Hania • Nea Roumata • Agia Irini • Epanohori • Sougia • Omalos • Lakki • Fournes • Hania

159km/99mi; under 4 hours' driving; Exit B from Hania (plan page 8). Coming back down from Omalos you may well meet coaches — patience and care are required.

Walks en route: Walks 1, 2, 16, 17, 19-21

Picnic suggestions (see pages 10-13): 1 at Agia Lake, 16 at the Agia Irini Gorge, 17 at Sougia

This tour takes a very picturesque route through wooded valleys and the Agia Irini Gorge to Sougia, a pleasant backwater. En route one or some of your company might like to walk down the gorge (Walk 16) and meet up in Sougia. At Sougia, you may like to do the very attractive walk along another gorge to the site at Lisos, and then swim in the lovely clear water from Sougia's pebbly beach, before heading into the hills. The stretch to Omalos on the return journey is one of the most beautiful parts of the tour. So even if you're not going to 'walk Samaria', this tour will take you to the top — where shepherds gather on the plain and griffon vultures soar overhead.

Leave Hania as for Car tour 1 on page 16 and turn left for 'National Highway/OMALOS' at the wide Y-fork. Drive under the A90 highway and through the suburb of **Vamvakopoulo** (🛏), and then **Agia** (10km), setting for Walk 1 and a lovely place to picnic. Continue until you see the right turn for 'SOUGIA' and 'SKINES' (12 km; opposite a 🛏 and a war memorial). Take this turn and cross the bridge over the Keritis River. The road bypasses first Alikianos and then Skines. Once through **Hilaro** (20km) it won't be long before you are driving through wooded valleys, planted with citrus trees.

The road starts to climb seriously (22km) and becomes more twisty as it leads through the foothills of the White Mountains. Pass through **Nea Roumata** (29.5km) and **Prases** (30km 🛏✖). Glorious hillsides surround you now — covered in chestnut, fig, olive, walnut and plane trees ... to name but a few. Pass the turning left for Omalos (38.5km).

Just beyond this turning, the Agia Irini Valley begins on the left; it runs through a gorge and down to the Libyan Sea, emerging at Sougia. Enter **Agia Irini** (42km; 🛏 at 43km, not open Sundays). After you leave this village (a sign tells you so at 44km), watch for a board on the left announcing the Irini Gorge (Walk 16) — you may like to park there and enjoy a picnic in the pines.

Pass through **Epanohori** (45.5km), from where you will have a first glimpse of the Libyan Sea, and start heading down to Sougia — via **Prines**, **Tsiskiana** and **Kambanos** (52km), beyond which the road swings round left and continues through **Maranes** and **Agriles**

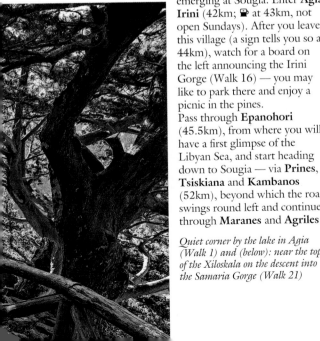

Quiet corner by the lake in Agia (Walk 1) and (below): near the top of the Xiloskala on the descent into the Samaria Gorge (Walk 21)

View to Lakki

(56km; 🍴, not open Sundays). Turn left at the T-junction one kilometre past Agriles (Paleohora is off to the right — 22km away). In a kilometre or two you will have a splendid view over the valley and down to the sea, tucked neatly into the V ahead. **Moni** is the last village before **Sougia** (67km). Walk 16 ends in this backwater, and Walk 17 begins here. Our suggested picnic spot for Sougia, shown on page 89, is only 10-15 minutes away on foot.

Head back from Sougia the same way (via Moni, Agriles and Agia Irini) and after 29km take the turning for Omalos passed earlier. Some 9km along, as you drive through a pass, the road goes by a small white church on the right. Keep right at a fork by a *cafeneion* sign; by now you will be on the **Omalos**. You reach the road which leads along the side of the plain to the top of the Samaria Gorge at a T-junction by the inviting-looking Agriorodo Villas. Turn right and drive to the **Xiloskala** at the top of the ravine. From here you can look down into the gorge

itself (Walk 21) and up to Gingilos Mountain (Walk 19; photographs pages 93 and 98). You'll also see the route up to the mountain refuge at Kallergi, which we follow at the start of Walk 20. We hope this panorama will inspire you to walk!

From the Xiloskala keep on the main road back to Hania, about an hour's drive away. In pretty **Omalos** (⛰🍴) you pass the Hotel Neos Omalos at the edge of the plain. Coach groups stop here for breakfast, en route for Samaria.

Leave the plain behind and start to descend towards the distant coast. The most noticeable place on the return route is **Lakki** (127km 📷🍴), shown above. Take care past here to follow the road round to the right (132km) near the turning to Askordalos. Drive into **Fournes** (🍴), go over the bridge and curve left through the village. Pass the junction to Alikianos, and go straight on (🍴 145km). After 8km you drive under the national highway and soon meet the turning right, back to the centre of **Hania** (159km).

Car tour 4: THE AKROTIRI PENINSULA

Hania • Kounoupidiana • Stavros • Agia Triada • Moni Gouverneto • (Souda Bay Cemetery) • Hania

50km/31mi; 2 hours' driving; Exit C from Hania (plan page 8). Note: The Gouverneto Monastery is closed from 14.00-17.00, but the powers that be often close from 12.00. *Men should wear trousers and women longish skirts.*
Walk en route: 10
Picnic suggestion (see pages 10-13): CT4 at Moni Gouverneto

The Akrotiri Peninsula, mushrooming out into the sea northeast of Hania, invites exploration. You may have seen some of it if you flew into Hania's airport, but you won't have seen any of the peninsula's treasures. The ruins of what is purported to be the island's earliest monastery are accessible by foot from this tour — as well as two other monasteries. All three are in lovely settings. With splendid views and swimming possibilities, this short tour could well fill a whole day very pleasantly.

Leave Hania by Exit C (El Venizelou): 1.5km from the market, follow the road round to the right, just beyond the Doma Hotel. The road, signed for the 'AIRPORT/VENIZELOS' TOMBS', climbs up out of Hania, leaving the old part of town (Halepa) off to the left. The left turn you need to take to get out onto the peninsula comes up at 5km at a rather odd junction — a roundabout set off to the left: first go left for the 'VENIZELOS' GRAVES', then take the first right for 'KOUNOUPIDIANA'. But for a wonderful view of Hania, first detour *left* instead of right at this roundabout and drive for two minutes to the Venizelos' Graves, where you can gaze down over the town, the north coast, and Theodorou Island beyond (📷).

Staying on the main route, very soon after the roundabout you will have another good view (📷) across Akrotiri to Stavros, where the mountain falls away into the sea. Coming to a large

Y-fork (7km ☕), take the right arm, then keep left and start heading downhill, through **Kounoupidiana** (✗). As you leave the village, turn left at 8km for Stavros. **Kalathas Beach** (9km ✗) is passed, followed by **Horafakia**. About 0.5km beyond the latter, turn left for Stavros. Three kilometres further on, turn right at a junction and come into **Stavros** (✗); the lovely beach, shown above, is perfect for swimming and picnicking.

Now head back the way you

Children at a remembrance service

Above: Stavros, where the mountain falls into the sea and the beach is perfect for a swim and a picnic. 'Zorba the Greek' was filmed here. Left: flower-bound house outside Hania

came, as far as the fork in **Horafakia** (20km). Instead of going right, back to Hania, take the left-hand turning (signposted 'AG TRIADA MONASTERY'). At the next fork (20.5km) head left (same signposting), heading towards the mast on the hill ahead. Turn left at the next set of signs (23.5km) — one pointing in the direction you've come from Horafakia, the other right to Hania (but no sign pointing left at time of writing). Drive down the avenue of trees to **Moni Agia Triada★** (24km ♣✕).

After visiting the monastery, head on to Gouverneto, four kilometres away. With your back to Agia Triada, go right. A sign for Gouverneto (ΓΟΥΒΕΡ–ΝΕΤΟ) takes you into a right turn at 25km. Apart from visiting **Moni Gouverneto★** (29km ♣), why not picnic on the nearby slopes (Picnic CT4) or follow Walk 10 down to ancient Moni Katholikou, shown on page 25?

Return to Agia Triada and, at the junction beyond the monastery (34km), go left for Hania. A kilometre further on, turn right; the road, signposted to Hania, curves round to the left. Half a kilometre along, turn right and then right again (38km). Where the road divides above Souda Bay (43km), either go left and down via the Souda Bay Cemetery and Souda or continue straight to **Hania** (50km).

Car tour 5: THE FOOTHILLS OF THE LEVKA ORI (THE WHITE MOUNTAINS)

Hania • Aptera • Katohori • Kambi • Mournies • Hania

67km/42mi; 2 hours' driving; Exit A from Hania (town plan page 8). Good roads throughout.
Walks en route: 3, 4

Picnic suggestions (see pages 10-13): 3 at Katohori or in the Diktamos Gorge, 4 just outside Kambi

History and hills combine nicely on this tour, which is a short spin into the lovely countryside inland from Hania. With the wild flowers of spring, the stillness of high summer or the colours of autumn, it's a pleasant morning or afternoon circuit. You'll drive to the fringe of the Levka Ori — often snow-capped until mid-summer.

Leave Hania by Exit A (Apokoronou; 🚍). At the traffic lights at the end of this avenue, go straight on for 'RETHIMNON'. Then keep following signposting to Rethimnon, to eventually join the A90 national highway in the direction of Rethimnon.

Make the first move off the beaten track by turning right for 'APTERA' at 12km. At a junction after 1km (in an area called **Megala Horafia**, although it may not be signed as such) bear left at a brown sign for 'ANCIENT APTERA'. After one kilometre you will see **Aptera★** (🏛) spread out to the right. Drive on to the Turkish fort perched up in a commanding position over Souda Bay (15km 📷).

From the fort go back to the junction in **Megala Horafia** and turn sharp left for Stilos, heading down through undulating hills. Make another sharp turn, this time to the right, at 20km ('MALAXA'). Beyond **Malaxa**, at 29km, turn left for Kontopoula. (Turning *right* at this point, you would find a good taverna with magnificent views a minute away; ✕📷.) Head on to **Kontopoula** — a gorgeous panorama of hills and mountains is ahead.

At the Y-fork not far past Kontopoula, keep left into the next collection of houses on the route, **Katohori** (34km). At the far end of this village, turn left over the bridge (signpost: 'VOLIKAS SHELTER/MADARO/KAMPOI'. Walk 3 starts here by the bridge, and you can park here to try either suggestion for Picnic 3 (there's a photo of the gorge on page 51).

Now make for **Kambi** (38km) and take the right-hand fork into the village square. The church and a *cafeneion* are on the right. Walk 4 is based here, and a 10-minute stroll along that route would take you to a lovely picnic setting.

Return the way you came; beyond the bridge at Katohori turn left instead of right. At the junction in **Gerolakos** (47km) turn right. Past **Loulos**, **Aletrouvari** and **Panagia** (where you pass a war memorial on the left), the route curves down the side of a steep valley, through **Vantes** and **Mournies** (62km). Now just keep ahead under the A90 national highway and then straight on in the one-way system to **Hania**'s market (67km).

Car tour 6: A SLICE OF CRETE

Hania • Vrises • Askyfou • Hora Sfakion • Frangokastello • Selia • Asomatos • Moni Preveli • Rethimnon • Georgioupoli • Hania

240km/149mi (via the old road from Rethimnon); 223km/138mi (via the A90 national highway from Rethimnon); 6-7 hours' driving; Exit A from Hania (town plan page 8). The road south, although it has undergone widening, is a mass of tortuous loops. Special care is needed when taking bends or overtaking (if you ever get the chance), because there are a lot of buses and coaches on this route. Fortunately their drivers are experienced! Note:

Moni Preveli is open from 08.00-13.00 and from 15.00 to 18.00; men should wear trousers and women longish skirts.

Walks en route: 2, 5, 6, 8, (9), 24, 25, 26, 27
Picnic suggestions (see pages 10-13): 6 at Kournas Lake, (8a or 8b near Rethimnon, 9 in the Myli Gorge), 25 in the Imbros Gorge, 27 by the arched bridge over the Megalopotamos River, CT6 in the Kourtaliotiko Gorge

You'll sample a bit of everything on this tour, which encompasses a neat square of the island. First we head south, following the same route thousands of retreating, war-weary Antipodean and British soldiers trudged over during World War II. We call in at the pretty harbour village of Hora Sfakion, from where boats ply west to Loutro, Agia Roumeli at the foot of the Samaria Gorge, and Paleohora. We turn east, following the coast to Frangokastello, a solitary landmark, once a fortified castle. Past the Kotsifou Gorge, we visit one of Crete's most beautiful monasteries, Moni Preveli, set in glorious solitude. Heading north to Rethimnon, we leave the views over the Libyan Sea, following the Kourtaliotiko Gorge. Here it's really worth getting out of the car to walk down to a magical spot where there is a waterfall and a small church tucked away. From Rethimnon it's back to base — either via the old country road through Episkopi or along the direct A90 national highway.

Leave Hania by Exit A (Apoko-ronou; ☎). At the traffic lights at the end of this avenue, go straight on for 'RETHIMNON'. Then keep following sign-posting to Rethimnon, to eventually join the A90 national highway in the direction of Rethimnon. Pass the turning off to Aptera★ (12km; Car tour 5). At 30km turn right towards 'VRISSES'. Turn right at the T-junction, then left. After 1km, in

Vrises (31km) you come to a three-way fork: take the middle route and head south, with the magnificent White Mountains lying to the right. Keep following 'Sfakia', going left at a Y-fork after 750m and right at the following T-junction. You soon pass the left turn to Alikampos (37km).
The road twists uphill, the landscape becoming rockier and greyer with the climb. There's a

splendid sight as you round a corner (47km 📷): the plain of Askyfou, shown on page 16, spreads out across to the left of the road. A striking Turkish fort sits on a mound in the foreground. **Kares** (48km; Walk 26) is the little village on the hillock down to the left. The road hems the plain, and the next village is the main one of the area, **Askyfou** itself (49km 🍴). Drive on round the plain and then follow the road as it heads south again. This is the route that thousands of soldiers from Britain, Australia and New Zealand took when fleeing Western Crete.

The road skirts the Imbros Gorge, which you see down left at 55km. Walk 25 starts here; a shortish walk from **Imbros** would take you to the pretty picnic spot shown on page 113 (left) — or there are pine-shaded picnic areas in the gorge itself (paid entry). Shortly (at 59km), if you look left again, you can see along the south coast to the east — including Frangokastello. But you are still high up above the sea and need to drive carefully as the road snakes its way down to the coast in loop after loop. At 68km, the coast road comes in from the east. Continue down and on into the pretty village shown on page 111, **Hora Sfakion★** (72km 🏨✕). As you curve down into the village, take the lower road to the harbour. Walks 21-25 finish at Hora Sfakion — by boat or on foot. Head back out the way you came in and, at a Y-fork 3km uphill, follow a sign for 'FRAGO-KASTELLO' [sic] straight on along the coast. Pass through **Komitades** (76km); Walk 25 — which started out at Imbros — can end here at Komitades, or at Hora Sfakion. Continue on through **Vraskas**, **Vouvas**, **Nomikiana** and **Agios Nektarios** (where Walk 26 ends); then turn right at 83km for Frangokastello, heading down towards the sea. After wandering round the ruined castle at **Frangokastello★** (87km 🏰; photograph page 30), carry on along the same coast road, still heading east. Turn left at the T-junction (90km), where a sign points right to 'Rethimnon 55km', but nothing is signed to the left (at time of writing). Drive through **Skaloti** and on to **Argoules**. Cross a stream and come into **Ano Rodakino** and **Kato Rodakino** (100km).

Beyond the right-hand turn to Koraka Beach, the views are well worth stopping to admire. There is a particularly good viewpoint looking back west along the coast at 103km, and you can park at 104km to admire the panorama (📷): steep cliffs plunge down to the sea on your right, and the inland landscape is dramatically rocky and barren. A few kilometres

Mountains near Imbros

Castle and beach at Frangokastello; below: Plakias beach (Walk 2)

further on you have views in all directions … but nowhere to park.

The road bends down through **Selia** (111km). At 112km, take the sharp right turn downhill (the road from Rethimnon, skirting the Kotsifou Gorge, setting for Walk 2). From **Mirthios** (114km 🍴✕) there is a fine view over Plakias. Turn left at the junction where a sign points right to 'Plakias 3km' (115km). (But turn right here

for Walk 2 or to swim or have a taverna lunch at Plakias Beach.) Then pass **Mariou**, set well up away from the sea; flat, cultivated land is on your right.

If you decide not to visit the Preveli Monastery (which would be a great pity), you will find Rethimnon signposted at **Asomatos** (122km 🚌). Here the main tour turns down sharp right into a bend; you will be heading almost back on yourself (there is a signpost here for the monastery and Plakias). After 1.5km turn left on a tarmac road which you will follow all the way to the monastery. To the left you see the Kourtaliotiko Gorge. Soon you pass an eye-catching arched bridge; Walk 27 begins and ends here, and the surrounds are pleasant for picnicking. Keep going, past the ruins of the original 16th-century monastery★. Soon, just round a corner, over the hill, **Moni Preveli★** (129km 🛉) comes into view. The setting, shown on page 118, is beautiful and very peaceful. Below the monastery the Megalopotamos River opens out into the sea at a palm-fringed beach (photograph page 120). Walk 27 is a superb circuit via Preveli.

The tour continues from Preveli by retracing the route past the original monastery and arched bridge to the main road (135km). Turn right, back to **Asomatos** (136km), then turn right again, for Rethimnon.

This route takes you along the **Kourtaliotiko Gorge** for a short way. After 600m, you could pull into a parking bay, then walk ahead for 100m to a rock archway from where a path descends to the church of Agios Nikolaos and a splashing cool waterfall (Picnic CT6). Do make the effort to walk down — and back up. If you're lucky there won't be a coachload of other visitors.

From here head north. The countryside opens out at **Koxare** (143km). When you meet the main Rethimnon/ Agia Galini road (144km), turn left (🚍 151km). Pass a turning left to Hora Sfakion and continue into **Armeni** (157km 🚍). Before long the sea and the north coast are in sight in the distance and, as you approach Rethimnon, there is a very good view over the town and the New Harbour (📷). To explore **Rethimnon★** (167km 🍴 ⛱ ✕🚍⊕**M**) go under the national highway and follow the road round, first to the left and then to the right, to park in the town centre (plan page 9). The old harbour is a good place to stretch your legs. More than any other town on Crete, this still speaks of its medieval past, with its Ottoman and Venetian buildings. The museum houses a collection of coins and antiquities.

Leaving Rethimnon, make your way back onto the highway or, if you've still got some energy, follow us: go over the highway at large junction at the west end of Rethimnon, following *blue* signs for 'ATSIPOPOULO' and 'UNIVERSITY OF CRETE' (171km). Heading south, you

Left: Georgioupoli: a peaceful sight at the end of a rocky breakwater which protects the town beach to the right and the small harbour to the left (Walks 5 and 6). Right: the 'Old Mill' above Plakias (Walk 2)

will drive through **Atsipopoulo**, **Prines**, **Gonia** and **Agios Andreas** in quick succession — country villages set along a wooded valley. **Episkopi** (189km 🚲) is rather larger. Ignore a turning to Filaki; keep ahead and, in **Dramia** (193km), go sharp left (*not* signposted). Keep straight on when Filaki is indicated left again. There is a pretty church at the beginning of **Kournas** village (196km ✝🚲), before you climb up through the village square. As you leave Kournas, you will see the north coast again, and then Crete's only natural freshwater lake will come into view below — the lovely, invigorating sight shown on pages 60-61 (198km; Walk 6), with several good picnic spots.

Pass the end of the lake and follow signs to Hania. Turn left for Hania at the T-junction (203km) and drive a short way alongside the national highway. The road then crosses over the

32

highway, to come into the main square of **Georgioupoli** (204km ⛺ ✕). Walk 5 makes a pleasing circuit from this village to Selia and back (photograph page 56); Walk 6, another circuit, starts here, too, and visits Lake Kournas. Turn left at the Y-fork with a paved seating area in the middle, then go left again. This avenue of eucalyptus trees runs along at the right of the highway. Watch, after 5km, for where you can join the highway (*no* signposting at time of checking, but there is a large beflagged factory on the right). Turn right for Hania. Pass the Venetian fort that is now a prison known by its Turkish name, Itzedin, and continue to **Hania** (240km). Leave the highway after the large 'Mara-kaki' building, where Hania and Souda are signposted on *green*, then turn left at the junction and go back to town the way you came out.

Car tour 7: CRETAN TREASURES

Hania • (Rethimnon) • Armeni • Spili • Agia Galini • Festos • Agia Triada • Hania

264km/164mi; about 6 hours' driving; Exit A from Hania (see town plan page 8). This tour follows major roads all the way. Walk en route: (8, 9), 29

Picnic suggestions (see pages 10-13): (8 near Rethimnon, 9 in the Myli Gorge; at the Minoan sites of Festos and Agia Triada

Well, this *is* a long haul, but it takes in a very large slice of Cretan landscape on the way to its goals, Festos and Agia Triada. We've included it because we are sure that many of you will want to make the effort to see two of Crete's major sites, even though you are based in Western Crete. To reach our destination, we travel via Spili — an exceedingly picturesque spot — and then between Mt Kedros and Siderotas.

Leave Hania by Exit A (Apokoronou; 🚗). At the traffic lights at the end of this avenue, go straight on for 'RETHIMNON'. Then keep following signposting to Rethimnon, to eventually join the A90 national highway in the direction of Rethimnon. Pass the turnings to Aptera★ (12km; Car tour 5), Vrises and Hora Sfakion (30km; Car tour 6), and Georgioupoli (33km; also Car tour 6). The road runs directly along by the sea from here to Rethimnon (🚗 at 41 km; ✕🚗 at 48km). You

will have a good view of Rethimnon from the outskirts. Leave the highway at the exit for 'SPILI' (green board).
Head south now, through **Armeni** (70km 🚗 and nearby Minoan cemetery ⏸★), **Mixorouma** (86km 🚗; base for Walk 29) and **Spili** (89km ▲▲✕), a large and pretty village well worth a 'pit stop'. Continue via **Kisou Kampos** (95km 🚗) and **Akoumia** (98km), where the road doubles back on itself briefly. Look up to Psiloritis — which is quite likely to be snow-

Agia Galini is a very popular tourist centre, so try to visit out of season.

Festos and the Mesara Plain

capped until high summer. Take a moment, too, to admire the whole Ida range (☞), with Mt Kedros in the foreground.

Take the turning right to **Agia Galini** at 112km. The road divides: go left and drive down to the harbour of this busy resort (114km 🛥 ✕ 🍴). Having stretched your legs, head back to the main road. Keep ahead (right) at the junction, following signposting to Iraklion (△✕ at 116km). At 122km you drive into the county of Iraklion, past a mass of plastic greenhouses, and then on via the ugly, functional spread of **Timbaki** (127km 🍴). The main road sweeps around to the right and before long you will see a sign

indicating that Festos is 2km to the right.

The Minoan site of **Festos★** (129km 🚻 ✕ WC) is in a glorious position — with views towards the Dikti and Lasithi mountains to the east, the Ida range to the north, and the Asterousias to the south.

From Festos, carry on through the car park and fork right. This turning takes you back towards the Mesara Plain, to a spot from which you can walk down to **Agia Triada★** (132km 🚻) in a few minutes. The remains of this Minoan summer palace are also in a delightful setting.

When it's time to head for home, simply retrace the route back to **Hania** (264km).

Car tour 8: THE AMARI VALLEY

Hania • Rethimnon • Apostoli • Thronos • Fourfouras • Agios Ioannis • Gerakari • Rethimnon • Hania

240km/149mi; 6 hours' driving; Exit A from Hania (see plan page 8). Reasonable asphalted country roads, but they are narrow in places.
Walks en route: 7, 8, (9), 28

(Walks 29, 30 and 31 are nearby)
Picnic suggestions (see pages 10-13): (8 in Rethimnon, 9 in the Myli Gorge), 28 near Ano Meros, Amari Valley (CT8)

The Amari Valley forms a natural route from the north to the south and so was much used as a refuge during the Second World War. Encircled by some forty villages and dotted with Byzantine churches, the valley offers up lovely countryside along our immediate route. But we also enjoy awe-inspiring, sweeping views encompassing the southwest slopes of Psiloritis, Crete's highest peak, and the string of mountains formed by Kedros, Soros, Fortetza and Vrissinas.

Follow Car tour 7 (page 33) to **Rethimnon**, but *pass* the turn off to Spili, which is taken in Car tour 7. Take the *next* exit, following signs for 'AMARI' and 'PRASIES'. As you travel towards Prasies, looking southwest, you will see Vrissinas, the highest peak across the valley; if you would like to explore the summit one day, see the footnote on page 67. **Prasies** (71km ✝) is very pretty and shows signs of its Venetian past. Beyond the village, at the top of a ridge (72km), you enjoy a spectacular view (📷) towards the Prassanos Gorge. Soon, just past the turning right to Mirthios, you pass the starting point for Walk 7, which explores this gorge.
At a Y-fork before the **Potamon Dam**, go left. The road edges the dam (keep following 'APOSTOLI'; ✖🍴), then comes into **Apostoli** (90km ✝✖ and 🍴 just beyond the village). This village is at the head of the Amari Valley, and our circuit will bring you back to this point. Keep straight on through **Agia Fotini** (91km 🍴) and stay

on the main road until, on a bend, you see a sign for **Thronos**. It leads you left and up to the village (92km ✝). After visiting the 14th-century church of Panagia, return to the main road and turn left, continuing the circuit. Pass below Kalogeros (✝ with 14th-century frescoes), a pretty hillside village set up to the left of the road, and — a minute beyond here — look right to see the small 15th-century Byzantine church of Agia Paraskevi.
Pass the junction (93.5km) to Amari and keep straight on the main road (🍴 97km) as it curves left. Go through **Afratas** (100km) and continue through groves of ancient olive trees, with fine views right towards Amari. Then come into **Visari** (103km). The road curls round the edge of the village and heads up to **Fourfouras** (105km 🍴), which is mainly set down to the right of the road. Behind Fourfouras lies Mt Kedros (1777m/5830ft) — a very comfortable mound, compared to the tantalising jagged teeth and high

The Amari Valley

slopes of Psiloritis to the left of the road. Two kilometres past Fourfouras, as you continue to climb, look right and back over the village and the entire basin of the Amari Valley below you (📷).

Drive on via **Kouroutes** (112km ✝) and **Nithavris** (116km). Here, at the end of the village, turn right (by a war memorial) towards Agios Ioannis. This route cuts across the valley and goes through the upper part of **Agios Ioannis** (120km). *Be sure to follow a hairpin bend round to the right* at 120.5km (*don't go straight ahead for Agia Paraskevi*). This bend now takes you through the lower part of Agios Ioannis. As you cross a bridge (125.5km) over the River Platys look right to see the picturesque old bridge shown on page 12 (Picnic CT8). Past the bridge, the road starts to climb up the west side of the valley, above the olive tree line. Go through **Hordaki** (132km) in moments and **Ano Meros** (136km),

36

where Walk 28 starts and ends. You could follow the first 20 minutes of that walk to a lovely picnic spot by a chapel (see page 122). There's a striking war memorial at the far end of Ano Meros, portraying a woman with a hammer in her hand. Mt Samitos rises to the right of the small village of **Drigies** (138km). Move on through **Vrises** and **Kardaki** and then, just before Gerakari, keep watch on the right for the monastery of Agios Ioannis Theologos (✝), with 13th-century Byzantine frescoes. Even in autumn, **Gerakari** (145km) is visibly greener than the rest of the countryside. A cemetery on the left precedes **Meronas** (150km ✝), where fresh spring water pours down hillsides.

Turn left as you enter **Agia Fotini** (155km; *not* signposted) and go straight into **Apostoli**. You have now completed the valley circuit. Back in **Rethimnon**, join the A90 national highway and head west back to **Hania** (240km).

❀ Walking

Western Crete is certainly a walkers' paradise but, even if you aren't an avid walker, there are plenty of opportunities for gentle strolls and rambles in the depths of the country-side, where you will develop a real appreciation for this magnificent corner of Greece. So if you can't 'do Samaria', you *could* manage a good number of our walks.

The 'Landscapes' series is built around walks and excursions that can be made *in day trips* from your home base. So all the walks in this book were originally conceived as day excursions *accessible by bus* from Hania or Rethimnon. These days many people are keen to hire cars and would prefer circular walks. But the beautiful old donkey trails and mountain paths were built to take people and livestock from one place to another: they are all linear. One solution is to just walk part-way and return to your car. Another solution —where possible — is to walk from A to B and take a bus back to your car (or, to be on the safe side, drive to the end of the walk, leave your car there, and take a bus back to the start). Suitable walks (not necessarily circular) are indicated by a 🚍 symbol in the Contents. It may be one of the *variations* of the main walk that is recommended: look for the 🚍 symbol under 'Access' (with waypoints for the walk start so that you can set your satnav).

Do consider combining some of the walks by spending a night or two away from your hotel, thus making a patch-work of mountain, gorge and coastal paths (see Walks 16-26 for instance). Just a word of caution: *never try to get from one walk to another on uncharted terrain!* Only link up walks by following paths described in these notes or by using roads or tracks; don't try to cross rough country (which might be dangerous) or private land (where you might not have the right of way).

The people you meet are very much a part of the landscape, countryside and essence of Crete. Do greet anyone you pass or see working in a field when you are out walking. Please don't — perhaps through your natural reserve — pretend they don't exist!

There are walks in this book for everyone.

Beginners: Start on the walks graded ● or ●, and check all the short and alternative walks. The picnic suggestions on pages 10-13 offer a large selection of very easy walks.

37

Experienced walkers: If you are accustomed to rough terrain and are feeling fit, you should be able to enjoy all our walks. Many — especially those in gorges — require agility, and a couple will demand a head for heights as well. Take into account the season and weather conditions: don't attempt the more strenuous walks in high summer; protect yourself from the sun and carry ample water.

Experts: Head for the high mountains. Both the White Mountains and the Ida Range (Psiloritis) will be a great attraction for you (Walks 4, 19, 20, 30).

Grading, waymarking, maps, GPS

We've tried to give you a quick overview of each walk's **grade** in the Contents. But many of our walks have shorter or alternative versions! In the Contents we've only had space to show the *lowest* grade of a *main* walk: for full details, including easier versions, see the walk itself. Here is a brief overview of the four gradings:

● very easy — more or less level (perhaps with a short climb to a viewpoint); good surfaces underfoot; easily followed

● easy-moderate — ascents/descents of no more than about 300-500m/1000-1800ft; good surfaces underfoot; easily followed

● moderate-strenuous — ascents/descents may be over 500m/1800ft; variable surfaces underfoot — you must be sure-footed and agile; possible route-finding problems in poor visibility

● expert — only suitable for very experienced hillwalkers with a head for heights; hazards may include landslides or balancing on ledges or the narrow edges of watercourses with no respite from constant exposure

Any of the above grades may be followed by:

⁞ *possibility* of vertigo — for those with no head for heights at all
⁞⁞ *danger* of vertigo — you must have a very good head for heights

Assigning grades to walks is *very* subjective — and giving them a 'vertigo' rating even more so! Until you get used to Crete's terrain and know your 'vertigo tolerance', why not try walking with one of the many **guided groups**? Note also: should you wish to walk further afield, we suggest you contact the Alpine Club in Hania (www.eos hanion.gr; see plan on page 8) or the refuge at Kallergi (see 'Short walk' on page 97 and photograph on page 98).

It's always encouraging to see **waymarking** along the route. But, unless we specifically advise you to follow it, don't *rely* on the waymarking. You will also frequently come across parts of the 'E4' network of long-distance routes. These 'European Rambler Trails' are usually well waymarked with yellow flash paint marks and signposted with yellow and black triangular plaques (see photograph on page 90). Many of our walks follow the E4 for some or all of the way. To see the entire **E4 trail across Crete**, go to destinationcrete.gr, where you can find maps of all the segments, see them displayed on Google Maps and even download tracks.

The **maps** in this book are based on Openstreetmap mapping (see page 2), but have been very heavily annotated from our notes and GPS work in the field. We hope that these maps, which we have found to be *very* accurate on the ground, will be a boon to walkers. It is a pity that we have to reproduce them at only 1:50,000 to keep the book to a manageable size; quite a few walkers buy both the paperback *and* download our pdf files so that they can enlarge the maps. Otherwise, we recommend the widely available GPS-compatible Anavasi 1:25,000 maps.

Free **GPS track** downloads and **height profiles** are available for all our walks: see the Western Crete page on the Sunflower website. Please bear in mind, however, that GPS readings should *never* be relied upon as your sole reference point, as conditions can change overnight. *But even if you don't use GPS,* our maps are now so accurate that you can easily compare them with Google Maps on your smartphone and pinpoint your exact position. And it's great fun dragging our GPX files over Google Earth to preview the walks in advance!

Things that bite or sting

Dogs on Crete, in our experience, are full of bravado, but not vicious. They bark like fury — indeed, what would be the point of guarding livestock if they did not? — and they will approach you, seemingly full of evil intention. However, they will shy off if you continue unperturbed. 'El-la' is a useful word to know. It means 'come here', if spoken encouragingly, or 'come off it', when said in a slightly diffident tone. Use it encouragingly with the dogs, and they'll soon go away. If you carry a walking stick, keep it out of sight and don't use it threateningly. If dogs worry you, you may like to invest in a 'Dog Dazer' — an ultrasonic device which deters threatening dogs without harming them. These are widely available on the web.

In the autumn you may be startled by gunfire, but it's only **hunters** — invariably on Sundays and holidays — in pursuit of game. You'll doubtless see them dropping or throwing stones into bushes — Greek beating!

Have respect for **donkeys'** hind legs; it's highly unlikely they'll kick, but don't forget the possibility.

Snakes may be seen, and vipers have been identified on

Crete, but they keep a very low profile and are not widespread. Poisonous **spiders**, called 'rogalida', do exist on the island, but it's highly unlikely you'll even catch a glimpse of one, as they are burrowers. You're more likely to see **scorpions**; they are harmless, but their sting is painful. Like spiders and snakes, they are likely to be hiding under rocks and logs in the daytime hours. So if you move a rock, etc, to sit down, just have a look under it first.

People who are allergic to bee stings should always carry their medication. **Bees** abound in high summer, especially around water troughs and thyme bushes.

Although we've mentioned this collection of creatures, it's very doubtful indeed that you will encounter anything that would harm you.

What to take

If you're already on Crete when you find this book, and you haven't any special equipment such as a day rucksack or walking boots, you can still do many of the walks — or you can buy the basic equipment at one of the sports shops in Hania or Rethimnon. Don't attempt the more difficult walks without the proper gear. For each walk in the book, the *minimum* equipment is listed. Above all, you need thick-soled stout walking trainers or walking boots. *Ankle support* is advisable in your footwear — indeed *essential* on many of the walks, where the path descends steeply over loose stones. You may find the following checklist useful:

walking trainers or walking boots
long trousers, tight at the ankles
long-sleeved shirt (sun protection)
waterproof rain gear
telescopic walking stick(s)
mobile phone (**112 is the Europe-wide emergency number**)
water bottle, plastic plates, etc
tissues
sunhat, sunglasses, sun cream
plastic groundsheet

up-to-date bus timetable
windproof (zip opening)
bandages and plasters
extra pair of (long) socks
knives and openers
light jerseys (or similar)
antiseptic cream
whistle, torch, compass/gps
spare bootlaces
small rucksack
insect repellent

Please bear in mind that we've not done *every* walk in this book under *all* conditions. We might not realise, for example, just how hot or how exposed some walks might be. Beware of the sun and the effects of dehydration. Don't be deceived by cloud cover: you can still get sunburnt, especially on the back of your neck and legs. We rely on your good judgement to modify the 'equipment' list at the start of each walk according to the season.

Where to stay

We have used Hania as our walking base, since the majority of people stay there when visiting Western Crete. But we have taken into account those of you staying at Rethimnon, Kastelli-Kissamos, or along the south coast, and you will find that you can join many of the car tours without difficulty. Several walks will be on your doorstep, but check the bus timetables (pages 133-4) to make sure that those furthest from your base are practicable. Due to the size of the island, some of the walks require bus changes. Although this makes the day longer, it has the advantage that you see more of the countryside. To find rooms in small villages, enquire at the local tavernas and *cafeneions* about renting a bed for a night. An overnight stay at the comfortable, staffed mountain refuge at Kallergi (see page 98) is recommended for those of you wanting to experience the Levka Ori — or you could stay down on the Omalos plain.

Walkers' checklist

The following points cannot be stressed too often:
■ **At any time a walk may become unsafe** due to storm damage or bulldozing. If the route is not as described in this book, and your way ahead is not secure, do not attempt to continue.
■ **Never walk alone** — four is the best walking group.
■ **Transport** connections at the end of a walk are vital.
■ Proper **footwear** is essential.
■ **Warm clothing** is needed in the mountains; even in summer, take something appropriate with you, in case you are delayed.
■ **Mobile/smartphone, compass/gps, torch, whistle** weigh little, but might save your life.
■ **Extra food** and drink should be taken on long walks.
■ Always take a **sunhat** with you, and in summer a cover-up for your arms and legs as well.
■ A **stout stick** or **telescopic walking stick** is a help on rough terrain and to discourage the rare unfriendly dog.
■ Read and reread the **important note** on page 2 and the Country code on page 11, as well as guidelines on grade and equipment for each walk you plan to do.

Weather

April, May, September and October are perhaps the best months to walk on Crete. The air temperature is moderate, but the sun shines. It is possible to walk during

Moni Katholikou and the bridge over the gorge (Walk 10)

June, July and August, however, because although it may be very hot by the coast, there's often a light breeze in the mountains. There's no doubt it's more tiring though, and great care should be taken in the sun and heat. Walks offering little or no shade (for instance Walks 11, 22 or 24) should be undertaken in high summer *with caution*.

The *meltemi* blowing in from the north tends to be a bad-tempered wind, bringing strong, hot breezes in the height of summer. These breezes stir up the dust, move the air about, but don't really cool it.

During February and November it often rains. The months of December and January are chilly and, if it rains, it may do so for two or three days at a time. However, the winter in Crete brings an incredible clarity on sunny days and some really perfect walking weather, when temperatures may be around 20°C (68°F).

It's worth remarking, too, that more often than not, when it's windy along the north coast, it's calm on the south of the island.

Greek for walkers

In the major tourist areas you hardly need to know any Greek at all but, once you are out in the countryside, a few words of the language will be helpful. Anyhow, it's nice to be able to communicate — if only a little — and people will marvel at your attempts.

Here's one way to ask directions in Greek *and understand the answers you get!* First memorise the few 'key' questions given below. Then, always follow up your key question with a **second question demanding a yes (ne) or no (ochi) answer**. (By the way, Greeks invariably raise their heads to say 'no', which looks to us like the beginning of a 'yes'. And 'ochi' (no) might be pronounced as **o**-hee, **o**-shee or even **oi**-ee.)

Following are the two most likely situations in which you may have to use some Greek. The dots (...) show where you will fill in the name of your destination. The approximate pronunciation of place names is in the Index.

■ Asking the way
The key questions

English	Approximate Greek pronunciation
Good day, greetings (formal)	**Hair**-i-tay
Hello, hi (informal)	**Yas**-sas (plural); **Yia**-soo (singular)
Good morning/afternoon	Kah-lee-**may**-rah/Kah-lee-**spay**-rah
Please —	**Sas** pa-ra-ka-**loh** —
where is	pou ee-**nay**
the road that goes to ... ?	o **thro**-mo stoh ... ?
the footpath that goes to ... ?	ee mo-no-**pa**-ti stoh ... ?
the bus stop?	ee **sta**-ssis?
Many thanks.	Eff-hah-ree-**stoh** po-**li**.

Secondary question leading to a yes/no answer

English	Approximate Greek pronunciation
Is it here?	**Ee**-nay **etho**?
Is it there?	**Ee**-nay eh-**kee**?
Is it straight ahead?	**Ee**-nay kat-eff-**thia**?
Is it behind?	**Ee**-nay **pee**-so?
Is it to the right?	**Ee**-nay thex-**ya**?
Is it to the left?	**Ee**-nay aris-teh-**rah**?
Is it above?	**Ee**-nay eh-**pano**?
Is it below?	**Ee**-nay **kah**-to?

■ Asking a taxi driver to take you somewhere and return for you, or asking him to collect you somewhere

English	Approximate Greek pronunciation
Please —	**Sas** pa-ra-ka-**loh** —
would you take us to ... ?	tha **pah**-reh mas stoh ... ?
Come and pick us up	**El**-la na mas **pah**-reh-teh
from ... (place) at ... (time)*	apo ... stees ...*

Instead of memorising the hours of the day, simply point out on your watch the time you wish to be collected.

As you may need a taxi for some walks, why not ask your tour rep or hotel reception to find a driver who speaks English (many now do). We'd also recommend an inexpensive phrase book with easily-understood pronunciation hints, as well as a good selection of useful phrases.

By the way: it's unlikely that a map will mean anything to the older people you may meet en route. Doubtless, they will ask you '**Pooh pah**-tay?' — at the same time turning a hand over in the air, questioningly. It means 'Where are you going?', and quite a good answer is 'Stah voo-**na**', which means 'to the mountains'.

Organisation of the walks

The 31 main walks in this book are located in the parts of Western Crete most easily accessible by public transport, using Hania (or Rethimnon) as the base. We hope that even if you're staying somewhere else in the west, most will be within range — especially if you've hired a car. (Although the walking notes show bus departures from Hania, you will find more complete timetables on pages 133-134, including Rethimnon, Kastelli-Kissamos, etc.)

The book is set out so that you can plan walks easily — depending on how far you want to go, your abilities and equipment — and what time you are willing to get up in the morning! You might begin by considering the fold-out touring map inside the back cover of the book. Here you can see at a glance the overall terrain, the road network, and the general orientation of the walking maps in the text. Quickly flipping through the book, you'll find that there's at least one photograph for each walk.

Having selected one or two potential excursions from the map and the photographs, look over the planning information at the beginning of each walk description. Here you'll find distance/hours, grade, equipment, and access. If the walk sounds beyond your ability or fitness, check to see if there's a shorter or alternative version. We've tried to provide walking opportunities less demanding of agility wherever possible.

When you are on your walk, you will find that the text begins with a general introduction and then quickly turns to a detailed description of the route itself. As well as distances, *times* are given for reaching certain points in the walk. Once you've done one walk, you'll be able to compare our very steady pace with your own; we hope you'll find we're in step, give or take! *Note that our times do not include any stops, so do allow for them.*

Below is a key to the symbols used on our large-scale walking maps.

▬▬▬ main road	E4 long-distance hiking route	start/end.waypoint
▬▬ secondary road	church, monastery. chapel	windmill.turbine
▭▭▭ 4WD track	cemetery.shrine	pylon.aerial
▬ rough track	factory	*P* picnic spot (see page 10)
------ footpath	bus stop.parking	best views
route of main walk and direction	spring, tank etc	page reference: map continuation
alternative route	ancient site	watermill.cave
other walk		

Walk 1: CIRCUIT VIA AGIA

See photographs on page 2, 13 and 22

Distance: 11km/6.8mi; 3h15min

Grade: ● straightforward walk on asphalt roads, with about 200m/ 650ft of ascents overall

Equipment: trainers, sunhat, picnic, water

Picnic: at Lake Agia

Access: any blue city 🚌 calling at Kato Stalos (not in the Timetables, but every 5-10 minutes); journey time 10min

Shorter walk: Kato Stalos — Agia (6km/3.7mi; 2h10min). ● Grade, equipment, access as above. Follow the main walk to Agia; return to Hania by Omalos 🚌 (Timetable 3), Sougia 🚌 (Timetable 6), or blue town 🚌.

Short walk: Agia — lake — Agia (1.7km/1mi; 35min). ● Easy, level walk. Access: 🚗 or Omalos 🚌 (Timetable 3), Sougia 🚌 (Timetable 6), or blue town 🚌 to the turning 'LAKE OF AGYIA' (35° 28.346'N, 23° 55.854'E) on the main road in Agia, where motorists can park. Take the turning. Soon, keep right at a fork. Pass a church on the left, cross a bridge with iron railings, then turn right to the lake. Return the same way.

● **Alternative walk: Agia — Platanias** (6km/3.7mi; 2h). Easy, mostly level walking; access as *Short walk;* equipment/ return as main walk. Follow the *Short walk* to the lake, then walk on to Kirtomados and pick up the main walk at the 2h-point.

Since we first walked here, much has been done to improve the lake at Agia as a recreational area (the new bridge shown on page 13 is an example), but so far it has escaped the more commercialised fate of Lake Kournas (Walk 6). Agia's lake (actually a man-made reservoir) is a particularly good place to watch birds, a lovely quiet oasis overlooked by the church of Saints Constandinos and Eleni — hence the name Agia ('holy'). This walk is all along asphalt country roads, but it is a welcome respite from the urbanisation around the coast, and the views to the Levkaa Ori (White Mountains) are stunning.

Start out at **Kato Stalos** (○): take the road signposted to STALOS. When it forks (**10min**; the national highway is visible up ahead) go left uphill, passing under the highway. At another fork, turn right towards PANO STALOS and follow the road across a small valley. Within a couple of minutes (**15min**) you will see on the left, across the valley, a lovely old house called **Metochi** (ⓐ). It is a classic example of the Turkish style of the 1700s. To its right, beyond

its garden, under two or three large trees, you may see a semi-circular hole in the wall. Water from the mountains, flowed through this hole into a stone pool. The water, having been used for washing clothes and people, was then drained into the valley to water the fruit trees.

Beyond a CEMETERY, keep up into the old village of **Stalos**, passing a few tavernas on the left. In the village centre, opposite a *cafeneion*, continue straight ahead (a right turn would lead to the church shown on page 2). Bear left at the next small square, leaving Stalos on a wide asphalted road, through olive groves. Ignore all turnings. The road climbs gently away from the coast, levels out, then starts to descend. You pass the small church of **Profitis Ilias** up to the left (**❶**); almost hidden by trees; **1h**). There is a fine panorama of countryside ahead as you continue along the road. Soon you may spot a church and graveyard below.

Before long you will see your destination down and across to your left. First of all a church comes into view; then you'll see the lake in the distance. Round the next bend, Kirtomados comes into range. Pass the first house in **Kirtomados** and, at the second house (on your right), take a CONCRETE TRACK (**❷**) left downhill between more houses. In the midst of the village, weave right and, at a junction of sorts (where there's a large mulberry tree on the left), turn left in front of a large old house with an arched wooden door. In 50m/yds, by a shady taverna on the right, turn left on the road.

At the next JUNCTION (**❸**), where there is a small shrine dedicated to **Agios Nektarios** off to the left of the signposts, follow the road round to the right.

Some **1h45min** en route, just before a bridge, take a track going left. In two minutes you will be at the edge of the LAKE. This is a very pretty place to picnic, but there is also a tastefully-finished 'birdwatchers' café'. Look out for terrapins,

too, basking on the rocks in summer.

If you are doing the Shorter walk, from here head back to the road, go left and continue to the main Hania road at **Agia**; both the blue city buses and the country buses stop opposite the end of this road coming from Kirtomados.

For the main walk, return the way you came to **Kirtomados** (**2h**). Pass the concrete track you took on your approach and the CHURCH, both on your right. Fork left past the church and within 100m/yds pass a WAR MEMORIAL (**❹**) on the right. Just 30m further on, at the edge of the village, turn right towards PLATANIAS (signposted in Greek; straight on is signposted to Platanias and Patelari.) There is a lovely view to the White Mountains on the left. Now just stay on this country road, ignoring any turnings.

The road starts to rise and you glimpse the **Patelari River** down to the left, through the trees. Five minutes later Patelari's two distinctive churches come into view on the left, across an orange grove. The road bends to the left and then right, and you can enjoy two to three minutes of plane tree-shade, with orange groves on the right. It is hard to believe that the hubbub of the coastal villages is so near.

Some 30 minutes from Kirtomados (**2h30min**) you pass the tiny church of **Ag Georgios** (**❺**) — known locally as 'Drunk George' — almost hidden in bougainvillea. It's usually locked. Then, five minutes later, you arrive at the lovely DRAKIANA RIVERSIDE

RESTAURANT on the left — a gloriously shady riverside taverna, a perfect place for a leisurely pit stop.

Having relaxed and eaten some delicious home-cooked food, continue on the road. Ten minutes from the taverna (where the road curves left and there is a mass of water pipes on the right), leave the road: go straight ahead on a ROUGHISH TRACK (**6**), the surface of which varies. Ignoring a minor crossing track and then a track to the left, follow this main track to the top of the hill, where the sea comes into view. Then, at a Y-fork, head left downhill. Ignore another fork off left, join an asphalt road after 350m/yds and follow it to the left. Just 100m further on turn off right, to walk under the national highway. Then walk straight ahead past PLATANIAS PARK and the large PRIMARY SCHOOL. When the road divides 200m past the school, curve round to the left. A minute later, turn right; after 100m/yds you will meet the main coast road in **Platanias**. Turn right; the BUS STOP (**O**; **3h15min**) is on your right.

Walk 2: KOTSIFOU GORGE

See photographs pages 30-31 and 32

Distance: 6km/3.7mi; 3-4h

Grade: ● adventurous, but suitable for anyone who is sure-footed and doesn't mind wading in *waist-deep* water at times (be prepared to get dirty, too). Ascent about 180m/600ft over-all. Not suitable after heavy rain

Equipment: bathing things and wading shoes, waterproof bag for camera, mobile, dry clothes/shoes, sunhat, picnic, water

Picnic: anywhere in the gorge

Access: 🚗 to/from Plakias (35° 11.423'N, 24° 23.714'E), or 🚌 from Rethimnon (Timetable 15); journey time 40min

Short walks

1 The 'Old Mill' and Mirthios (4.7km/3mi; 1h45min). ● Easy walk on tracks and paths, with about 170m/560ft of ascent. Stepping stones may prove difficult after rain. Trainers, sunhat, picnic, water. Access as main walk. Follow the main walk to the 'OLD MILL' (❻; **40min**), then take the signposted path to Mirthios — at first following the line of the aqueduct. After the path makes a U-turn to the right there's a nice view down to the tiny mill chapel. Then the path merges with a track, from where Plakias is visible down on the coast. Follow this track to the right for 50m, then, at a Y-fork, head right on a blue-waymarked trail (the path to the left may have a branch or log across it indicating 'not this way'). Contouring below a house, you come to a concreted T-junction, where you turn left, steeply uphill. At the next T-junction turn right to the old village WASHHOUSE in **Mirthios**. Just past it, take wide stone steps up past TAVERNA VRISI to the main village street and BUS STOP (❼; **1h15min**). After looking around and having some refreshment, head back to the WASHHOUSE and turn left, then immediately right. Follow this road all the way down to **Plakias (1h45min)**.

2 Old Mill (3.3km/2mi; 1h15min). ● Equipment/access/grade as Short walk 1, but only 50m/165ft of ascent. Follow the main walk to the 'OLD MILL' (❻; **40min**), then retrace steps to where you crossed on STEPPING STONES (❸). Keep straight on here, ignoring all turnings to the right, all the way

The popular walk to the 'Old Mill' above Plakias can be extended to make a real adventure. From the mill we continue upstream in the Kotsifou Gorge. There's no path, so much of the time you will be *in* the stream itself.

Start the walk at the BUS STOP (◯) in the centre of **Plakias**: follow the coastal road west towards the pier, crossing a BRIDGE over the mouth of the **Kotsifou Stream**. Take the next, narrow street to the right. At the junction after 250m/yds, turn hard right (signed to the youth hostel), recrossing the stream on another BRIDGE. The road bends left and passes the YOUTH HOSTEL (❶) and then a LIBRARY run by British ex-pats who are a great source of local information). By now there's gravel underfoot.

Keep straight on. Just over 500m past the library you come to a first old MILL(❷). (There

48

are three 16th-century Venetian mills in the gorge; we visit two on this walk; the third is further north.) This one has mostly collapsed, but parts of its impressive aqueduct remain. The village of Mirthios is visible up to the right from here.

Just under 100m past the mill turn left at a fork; then, 100m further on, go left at a Y-fork. Go left at the next fork, too, on a path down to a tiny field and then the stream (there is usually a cairn in the field marking the path to the stream). Cross the stream on STEPPING STONES (**3**) — tricky after heavy rain. On the far side, turn right on a track which narrows to a path. Carry straight on past an ARCHED BRIDGE (**4**) on the right — to a tiny whitewashed CHAPEL (**5**), partially built into the rock. There's a good view from here to the sea.

Return the 50m to the BRIDGE and cross it, then climb up to the second MILL — known as 'THE OLD MILL' (**6**; **40min**). This is a very substantial affair — you can see its walls rising above the vegetation. If you climb up and wander around the aqueduct, taking in the mill's layout, you may realise that this mill had a double function: water from the permanently flowing stream powered the grain-grinding apparatus on the upper floor, while the overflow water was used to wash wool or handwoven fabrics below.

Now walk back to the arched bridge, cross it and turn right. (*Short walk 2 goes left here.*) Descend into the stream. Now the fun begins. Depending on the time of year and seasonal rains, you may get *very* wet as you head upstream, wading and

clambering over rocks and boulders, sometimes dodging waterfalls, sometimes luxuriating in these 'power showers'.

Eventually you come to an old crumbled road. Follow this to a rusty manhole cover, then go left uphill on a path. At the point where the track is gated off, make a U-turn to the left. This brings you to the main road which you follow downhill to **Mirthios** (2h30-3h30min). After taking a break (perhaps in TAVERNA PLATEIA with its stunning views), walk a few metres further on, to the small parking area/BUS STOP. Then, opposite a gift shop, take broad steps down (past TAVERNA VRISI on the left) to the road. Turn left, then turn right immediately. On the descent a conical hill crowned by the remains of Plakias Castle can be glimpsed off to the east. All that is left of this Venetian fortress are the yellowish chapel walls. (During the Second World War, the Germans also appreciated the strategic significance of the bay, and the cliffs to the east are honeycombed with tunnels and gun turrets.) Regaining **Plakias**, retrace your steps to the BUS STOP (**O**; **3-4h**).

Walk 3: THE DIKTAMOS GORGE: FROM KATOHORI TO STILOS (OR NIO HORIO)

Distance: 9km/5.6mi; 3h35min to Stilos (10.4km/6.4mi; 4h to Nio Horio)
Grade: ● moderate-tough; way-marked gorge walk descending 250m/820ft; much clambering over boulders necessary
Equipment: walking trainers or boots, sunhat, picnic, water
Picnic: at the start of the walk or in the gorge
Access: Kambi 🚌 to Katohori (not in the timetables; departs Hania 14.00 Mon/Wed/Fri only); journey time 35min. Return on 🚌 from Stilos (not in the timetables; departs 16.45 in season; enquire locally); journey time 30min. Or 🚌 from Nio Horio (not in the timetables; departs 11.15, 13.10, 17.30 weekdays, 11.15, 16.20, 18.30 Saturdays/Sundays in season; enquire locally); journey time 30min

This is a very pleasant, but somewhat taxing walk through a glorious gorge. The bus ride from Hania is well worth the early start. The White Mountains rise in an awesome but splendid mass to one side as you climb into the foothills. The gorge is an attractive walking route, fringed with leafy plane trees and hemmed with pretty pink oleander bushes. The walk is demanding in many places, as the gorge floor offers every kind of surface underfoot. If you encounter any stock control gates, please re-fasten them after passing through.

The bus stops just before a BRIDGE (◉) on the south side of **Katohori**, where the road curves right (signposted to Madaro and Kambi). **To start the walk**, cross the road and walk straight on along a road signposted 'DIKTAMOS GORGE' (among others). The river bed that runs through the gorge to Stilos is down to your right. On the first big U bend to the left (sign: 'DIKTAMOS GORGE'), where there is a MINIATURE CONCRETE CHURCH, leave the main road and carry straight on, keeping downhill at any junctions. Pass a SMALL CHURCH on the right. Walk through a large square with a CHURCH on the left and a *cafeneion* on the right. Follow the 'DIKTAMOS GORGE' sign ahead — slightly left.
The road leads through orange

groves and soon passes a small PICNIC AREA on your right. Before the road crosses a concrete bridge, follow another large sign directing you left onto a dirt track. Almost immediately (after 15m/yds) drop down right into the stream bed (❶; RED PAINT ARROWS) and then out again, going through a STOCK GATE. Once through the gate, you are on a rough, rock-strewn path which follows the stream on your left. After 30m/yds, the

50

In the depths of the leafy Diktamos Gorge

path becomes more distinct and is lined with stones on both edges. It soon turns left through some large shrubs and continues along the stream. It crosses a smaller watercourse leading into the main stream and passes between two wooden benches. Just past the benches, go through another STOCK GATE and enter the main part of the **Diktamos Gorge**.

The route is waymarked with what can seem rather invasive large arrows, indicating the easiest walking route. It crosses and recrosses the river bed throughout the walk. There are many places to linger and picnic. In less than **1h** the landscape opens out somewhat; then the towering sides of the gorge close in on us again. In **1h30min** the route rises up to the left and there is a makeshift handrail to help you negotiate a steep drop.

By **3h** you are out of the gorge and walking along the river bed, as the countryside opens out. The walk continues in and beside the river bed. Five minutes later the waymarking leads us up to the right, away from the oleander-lined river bed and onto a MOTORABLE TRACK (**2**). In three-four minutes keep straight on, where a track goes off right. A minute later the

track divides; go straight on (**3**), on the right-hand side of the river bed. Just over 500m further on, the track goes back into the river bed for 50m, then heads up left, to a BRIDGE ON THE MAIN ROAD.

Once on the main road, turn right over the bridge, pass a SHRINE TO ST PANTELIMON and continue past the huge ETANAP Samaria water bottling plant, into **Stilos** (**3h35min**). There is a BUS STOP (**O**) opposite the large shady open area, outside a *cafeneion*. Rather than wait for the late afternoon bus, why not relax in the shade here for a while and then walk to **Nio Horio** just 25 minutes away (**4h**)? Here you can pick up one of the more frequent buses or a taxi. The BUS STOP is opposite the kiosk which you will see as you approach the village.

Walk 4: KAMBI • VOLIKA REFUGE • KAMBI

Distance: 14km/8.7mi; 4h55min

Grade: ● very strenuous, with a height difference of about 770m/2525ft

Equipment: walking boots, long trousers, long socks, windproof, sunhat, compass, picnic, water

Picnic: just outside Kambi

Access: 🚌 to/from Kambi; park near the church where the walk starts (35° 25.078'N, 24° 4.178'E).

There is a bus (see Walk 3) but times are not convenient and there is no same day return.

Alternative return: ● You could descend on the shepherds' dirt road from near the Volika hut. It winds gently downhill, with spectacular views over the coast. Beyond Madaro, you will be on asphalt until you reach Kambi. This descent adds 4km/2.5mi, making the walk 18km/11mi; under 6h.

If you have come to Crete prepared to spend some nights away from your base, consider staying in Kambi the night before starting this hike. It's a very pleasant, quiet village with a relaxed atmosphere. There is a bus up to Kambi at crack of dawn, but as this trek is a real energy-tester, you might find it helpful to be on the spot in the early morning ... particularly if you fancy turning it into an expedition.* As the success of this walk relies on compass readings (unless you are using our GPS files), do choose a clear day, when the mountains are easily visible and the views are sure to be good. The route up to Volika is now waymarked with E4 signs. Some are on poles, but many are large yellow, white and black circular 'poached eggs' painted on rocks. This has made the ascent and descent much easier, but it is still a good idea to use a compass or GPS and look out for the features mentioned in the description.

The bus stops in the square in **Kambi**, by the CHURCH. **Set off** (◉): walk right, past the church, on an asphalt road signposted to Madaro and the Volika Shelter. (The bus continues in the same direction towards Madaro.) Walk to the right of a defunct, vine-covered *cafeneion* and take a compass reading on the corner. Face the mountains towards which you are heading, which are due south, and notice, in particular, the tree-covered slopes of the ravine, which is south-southwest from this point. Then continue on the road, disregarding a track to the left passed a few minutes later. Pass a house that has rows of potted plants and flowers along its length, and a SHRINE — both on the right. Directly afterwards, at a junction, fork right on a road,

---

*You could hire a guide to show you the area *beyond* the Volika hut, which is our point of return. Taking your own provisions, you would stay overnight at the hut

(which is otherwise locked). You can arrange this via the EOS office at 90 Tzanakaki Street in Hania (tel: 28210 44647; www.eos hanion.gr).

following signposting for 'PSYCHRO PIGADI, THYMIA'. (There is also a signpost in Greek: 'Γερο Πρινος Ψυχρο Πηγαδι Θυμια'. At the next junction (①) go left between TWO OLIVE TREES and walk slightly uphill, towards houses on the edge of the village. Go right at the houses (now on a track, signposted in Greek to 'Βολικα') and then left at the next turn, past a VINEYARD. Down to the right is a PICNIC AREA, with a map.

The track runs out in front of a concrete farm building (**20min**). Take the signposted 'VOLIKA' footpath that leads steeply uphill here, guided by E4 waymarking. Initially there is fencing on the left, but very soon this stops. Fencing starts on the right, and your route runs quite near it. About five minutes from the start of the path, look out for a MAKESHIFT GATE. Notice a line of four low 'bumpy' hills on your left in the distance; the gate, set at an angle, is in line

View towards the Volika hut, on the final approach

with the second 'bump', and the barbed wire that has topped the fence breaks for the gate. Turn round here and get your bearings for the return. *This is important.* Beyond Souda Bay, in the distance, the Akrotiri airport mast is visible. At the left end of the same peninsula, where the mountainside seems to fall into the sea, is Stavros (shown on page 26). Further left, pick out the island of Theodorou, just off the north coast at Platanias and, beyond that, the Rodopou Peninsula. *Then take note of Kambi's position very carefully.* These precautions are to save you wading through thistles and thorny burnet on your way back down to the village.

Setting off again, your route continues uphill. You come up onto a track (where there is an asphalt road over to the right). Follow the track uphill and, 15 minutes later, as you round a bend, you will see the track bending left, cutting across a wooded ravine ahead. There is a stock control gate on the bend. From this point the mountains are spread before you, and this is a good place to get your bearings — you can see the

Volika hut up on the mountainside in the ravine you are aiming for, as well as the last curve of the track above Madaro (to the left of the hut).

Some 200m/yds after the bend, take the path striking off right uphill (❷; signpost: 'ΒΟΛΙΚΑ'). Five minutes later you will be at the TOP OF THIS RISE. Look ahead: there is one prominent, domed mountain which has trees down the left-hand side of its top. Two 'bumps' from that one, to the left, find a mountain with trees all over its summit. The route to the refuge is via the V-SHAPED RAVINE WITH TREES DOWN BOTH ITS SLOPING SIDES.

From the top of the rise continue by walking northnorthwest towards the ravine and the ascent route to Volika. After the top of the rise, head south towards a circular pasture area and scramble up some rocks to the right. Keep heading towards the ravine, going via more CIRCULAR PASTURES and keeping an eye out for the 'poached egg' waymarking. By **1h30min**, having negotiated some sharp, pale grey rock, you look up the ravine and towards

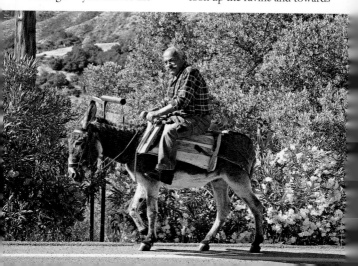

the final ascent. The good waymarking now leads you up the very steep right-hand side of the ravine. Trees provide shade and resting places. After climbing for 20 minutes or so, the path leads you to the other

(left) side of the ravine (**1h50min**). Ten minutes later it crosses back to the right. Some 35 minutes from starting up the ravine (**2h25min**), come to a flat wooded area: the ravine appears to end here, but follow the waymarking uphill.

The ravine becomes a gully, wedged in beside layered rock to the left of the route. Just under an hour from the start of the final ascent the Volika hut comes into sight. Five minutes later the path crosses the gully on the layered rock. Looking at your destination, approach it from the left to find easiest access. By **3h10min** you have the satisfaction of reaching the **Volika** HUT (**❸**). Apart from the new track — which is invasive right up here, but which has been made to aid shepherding — you feel miles from anywhere.

The return along your outward route should take much less time, although a large proportion of it requires careful walking and close attention to direction. It will take about an hour to get to the bottom of the ravine. Make your way back and, on the far side of the ravine, head due north — not northeast. Be sure to go far enough in a northerly direction before turning towards Kambi; wait until you can actually see the village and route on which you started the climb, before heading back down to **Kambi** (**❍**; **4h55min**). Or descend by the alternative route; this adds 4km, but the views are wonderful.

Walk 5: GEORGIOUPOLI CIRCUIT

See also photograph page 32
Distance: 14km/8.7mi;
4h15min
Grade: ● straightforward
climb/descent of 350m/1150ft,
but with some faint and
overgrown paths to locate and
negotiate; almost *no* shade
Equipment: walking trainers,
sunhat, picnic, water, swimming
things, long trousers/socks
Picnic: Georgioupoli harbour-
side, chapel shown on page 32
or beach (no shade); Exopolis

church (shade, benches)
Access: Rethimnon/Iraklion 🚌
(Timetables 1, 2) to/from Geor-
gioupoli; journey time 45min.
Or 🚗: park in Georgioupoli
Square (35° 21.770'N, 24° 15.588'E).
**Shorter walk: Circuit from
Argirimouri** (8km/5mi;
2h45min). ● Grade, equipment
as main walk. Access by 🚗 car:
park near Georgia's Taverna in
Argirimouri (35° 22.481'N,
24° 14.836'E) and pick up the walk
at the 45min-point.

Georgioupoli is a pleasant place for walking, eating,
swimming and relaxing. At the end of this walk, you
might like to cross the highway to the lake at Kournas
(Walk 6) for a swim or quiet lakeside taverna meal.

Start out at the GEORGIOUPOLI
BUS STOP (◉) on the A90
NATIONAL HIGHWAY. Cross the
road and take the road almost
opposite into **Georgioupoli**.

Follow the road straight across
the VILLAGE SQUARE and down
over a BRIDGE (❶) spanning the
fishing harbour. There's a lovely
view out to sea on your right

Left: view to the White Mountains and Exopolis (1h10min into the walk)

and up to the mountains on your left. Ignoring minor turns left and right, stay on this main road until you reach GEORGIA'S TAVERNA at **Argirimouri** (❷; **45min**). Turn right off the road here, walk in front of the taverna, and then take a single-lane road off left, just beside the taverna. (There is a hand-painted sign 'TO LIKOTINARA' on the stone wall.)

The asphalt road becomes a concrete track and climbs steeply (**50min**), past a large house on the left. After a couple more minutes, the concrete reverts to earthen track. Just ahead and slightly left, a stock control gate is labelled 'PATH TO LIKOTINARA'. Go through the gate and emerge in a small clearing. Ahead is a TREE WITH RED WAYMARKS and ROCKS WITH BLUE WAYMARKS; your path passes between the tree and rocks and winds uphill; *watch carefully for the occasional cairn,* as well as blue or red paint waymarks on the rocks.

After a few more minutes, pass through a STOCK CONTROL GATE in a fence (blue waymark). The path becomes more distinct and the views open out. In 10 minutes, there is a broken DRYSTONE WALL on your right. When the path splits, take the right-hand path, rising up alongside the wall. *Keep watch for cairns and occasional waymarks* as the path heads north-northeast up the hillside. As you are nearing the top, the path passes an old LIME PIT on the right.

The path rises to a TRACK (❸; **1h25min**), where you go left. After a few minutes the roofs of Likotinara come into view, and

the sea is seen to the right. Some 10-15 minutes later strike off right on a small concrete track which soon becomes a single-lane road, and head down towards Likotinara. In eight minutes, having wound through olive groves and past some old, ruined houses, you meet the road in **Likotinara** (**1h50min**). Turn right and walk to the VIEW-POINT (❹) over the coast and distant mountains. There is a monument here to Communist Resistance fighters.

Returning from the viewpoint, keep right along the village road past the turning where you came in. At the fork under 500m from the viewpoint, go left towards LITSARDA and VAMOS (Kefalas is signposted to the right). Pass a sign indicating you are leaving Likotinara and, eight minutes later, come to the start of **Selia** (**2h05min**). Follow the main road into the village, ignoring any turns left or right.

Then, opposite a BASKETBALL AREA and by a SHRINE at the corner of a house, turn left on a track (❺) (asphalted for the first 50m/yds). Follow it to a large house, and then turn imme-diately left on what is now an earthen track (blue waymark on the wall). In a couple of minutes go through a stock control gate, after which the dirt track continues to the left. Do *not* follow it; instead, as soon as you are through the gate, take the blue waymarked path downhill to the right. This path meanders down the hillside with occasional waymarks. In a few minutes, you will see the main asphalt road; just continue on the path, parallel with the road and slightly above it. Some

8

LandLandscapes of Western Cretenavigation>**58**   Landscapes of Western Crete

2h20min into the walk, you will see the sea again at Georgioupoli.

The path widens, as it comes down towards a HAIRPIN BEND in the road by a broken stone wall (**❻**; **2h25min**). Turn left here to continue on a wide dirt track.* In two minutes you will go through a stock control gate, followed quickly by another one as you head downhill. After another six or seven minutes, the dirt track ends in an OLIVE GROVE. Go straight ahead through the olive grove and find the best path you can down the hillside towards a SMALL FARM BUILDING beside the asphalt road. The path is *very* overgrown and prickly in places, but you need only persevere for about 300m/yds. If you *do* persevere with the path, you will walk past the front of the farm building, now apparently abandoned

(**2h50min**). The way becomes a concrete track and meets the main road.

Cross over and take the small road signed 'Exopolis'. Walk up to **Exopolis** (**3h**). When the narrow road forks, keep straight ahead (left). Then, at the T-junction, turn turn right, to pass the VILLAGE CHURCH (**❼**) on your right. This is a good place to stop for a break or a picnic, with benches in the shade and fine views.

From the church continue on the narrow road through the village houses and very soon you will see Georgioupoli down to the right. Follow the narrow road down to Georgia's Taverna *(the Shorter walk ends here)*. Now retrace your steps back to the bridge and then through **Georgioupoli** (**4h05min**), to the NATIONAL HIGHWAY and the BUS STOP (**❽**; **4h15min**).

*To avoid getting scratched when this track peters out after about 10 minutes, stick to the road from this hairpin bend. When you meet the road coming from Georgioupoli, turn left (right goes to Kalamitsa and Amigdali) and walk downhill for a few minutes, then turn right on the road signed to Exopoli, 1km away. Pick up the main walk now, at the 3h-point.

Walk 6: LAKE KOURNAS CIRCUIT

See also photograph page 32
Distance: 12km/7.6mi; 3h30min
Grade: ● easy-moderate; an easy
climb of 150m/500ft on an asphalt
road, then a gentle descent of
150m/ 500ft on dirt tracks.
Equipment: walking trainers,

sunhat, picnic, water, swimwear
Picnic: Lake Kournas
Access: Rethimnon/Iraklion 🚌
(Timetables 1, 2) to/from Geor-
gioupoli; journey time 45min.
Or 🚗: park in Georgioupoli
Square (35° 21.770'N, 24° 15.588'E).

This is a pleasant — fairly easy but longish — walk
through villages and countryside around the resort
area of Georgioupoli. The focal point is the lake at Kournas
— the only *natural* fresh-water lake on Crete (Lake Agia
visited on Walk 1 is a man-made reservoir).

Start out at the BUS STOP on the
A90 NATIONAL HIGHWAY (◉)
opposite the Georgioupoli turn-
off. Cross the road and walk
towards **Georgioupoli**. About
two minutes (150m/yds) from
the highway, and *before* you
reach Georgioupoli village centre,
turn sharp right (almost back on
yourself), following signposting
to 'RETHYMNO' and 'KOURNAS'.
Leaving Georgioupoli (**05min**),

and close to a petrol station,
continue on the main road
which swings right and
crosses over the highway by a
BRIDGE.
Once over the bridge, the road
swings left and you continue
along it, now parallel with the
highway. At a junction (**15min**),
there is a slip road left onto the
highway and a taverna ahead of
you. Follow your road around to

the right. At **20min** continue straight ahead towards 'Kavros' (**①**), *ignoring* a sign right to Lake Kournas. This road continues straight ahead through olive groves until it reaches the village of **Asprouliana** (**35min**). Shortly after walking past a new housing development, the old village begins. Opposite a FACTORY BUILDING on your left (**②**; **45min**), take a dirt track heading obliquely right. As you walk along this track through olive groves and fields, the White Mountains rise impressively ahead of you. About 10 minutes after starting on this track, ignore a track off to the left.

Eventually your track meets an asphalt road (**1h10min**). Turn right. About 10 minutes later, at a T-junction, turn left. Then turn right after just 40m/yds following signposting for Lake Kournas (**③**; **1h20min**), *noting this point for your return*. A couple of minutes later, at a T-junction, turn right between two buildings (again signed 'Lake Kournas'). In a few minutes, just by a BIRD-WATCHING HIDE, there is a footpath leading down to the edge of the lake (**1h35min**), a lovely place to picnic.

From here retrace your steps back to the junction at the 1h20min-point and now turn left for 'Georgioupoli'. Ignore tracks left and right into fields. (But after 250m/yds, you might like to turn left on a TRACK (**④**) and follow it as long as you like, for an even better view of the lake; the distance and time for this detour are *not* included in the main walk.

Eventually, turn left uphill on

asphalt at the sign for 'Mathes' (**1h50min**). As you ascend towards the village, the scenery begins to change from the flat coastal plain of the first half of the walk. You are soon edging a small ravine, pleasantly green and tree-covered.

Arriving in **Mathes** (**2h25min**), follow the main road through the village, passing the Mathes Taverna on your right and the main village CHURCH opposite the taverna on your left. Five minutes after leaving the village, and just after another CHURCH, the asphalt road makes a sharp hairpin bend to the right. Just before the apex of this bend, take the worn, NARROW DIRT TRACK (**⑤**) heading *downhill* on your left. (*Do not* take the dirt track leading left *up*hill just after the church and before this track.) Two minutes later, at a T-junction with a good dirt road, turn left.

This track meanders pleasantly through more olive groves before turning sharp right (where there is a house ahead; **3h05min**). About 100m/yds further on, the track forks. Take the left fork (**6**). As you arrive at the outskirts of Georgioupoli, the dirt track becomes a single-lane asphalt road. At a T-junction turn left (**3h15min**). The road soon bears round to the right and goes through a tunnel under the highway into **Georgioupoli**. At the next T-junction, turn right on the main road into the village. At the HOTEL DROSIA (**3h25min**) take the right fork towards the village centre. A short way along, at the T-junction with the main road through the village, turn right.

At the next junction, take the right fork, back to the BUS STOP on the NATIONAL HIGHWAY (**O**), where the walk began (**3h30min**).

Lake Kournas is a very popular recreationsal area with the locals and tourists alike. You can swim, rent pedaloes and other water sports equipment, laze about at a taverna … or feed the geese.

Walk 7: THE PRASSANOS GORGE

Distance: 10.6km/6.6mi; 3h30min *(allow a good 5h; see under 'Grade')*

Grade: ● moderate, but agility is required in a couple of places. Basically an overall descent of somewhat under 300m/1000ft.

Important notes: Outside high summer, if there has been a bad winter, or heavy rainfall, the gorge is not passable. To check the up-to-the-minute situation, contact staff at 'The Happy Walker', 56 Tobazi St, Rethimnon 28310 52920). This company also arranges good guided local countryside walks.

Or contact the Rethimnon Tourist Office on 28310 29148.

Equipment: walking trainers, sunhat, picnic, water

Picnic: anywhere in the gorge

Access: Rethimnon or Iraklion 🚌 (Timetables 1, 2) to the Rethimnon bus station; journey time 1h. Then take either a 🚕 taxi or an Amari 🚌 (not in the timetables, but departs 14.00 Mon/Wed/Fri *only*); journey time 30min. Ask for 'Prassanos' (the gorge) or Mirthios. Return on town 🚌 from Missiria (every 15min); journey time 30min

---

T his gorge is an awe-inspiring and inviting sight as it carves a swathe through the countryside to the coast by Rethimnon. It has obviously been created by great force — as you'll see from the massive boulders en route. The landscape around is very open and pleasing to look at, making a good, accessible walk.

The taxi or bus will drop you at a road junction where a sign indicates MIRTHIOS off to the right. From this junction (○), **start out** by walking about 100m/yds towards AMARI along the road. Then turn left on a concrete track. Immediately you are facing the huge entrance to the gorge; the landscape is tremendous here, open and grand. Just before the concrete runs out, in 50m/yds or so, open the wire gate and go through. You may see a sign on this gate or the next one indicating 'no entry': you can safely ignore this, *but please close and re-secure any gates!* (The farmer who owns the buildings a short way ahead has told us he put up the sign out of frustration with walkers who left gates open; he does not mind walkers who behave according to the country code.)

Continue down the track. Pass through a STOCK CONTROL GATE and walk to the left of the FARM BUILDINGS (**12min**), going straight over the 'yard' and passing through a SECOND STOCK CONTROL GATE. *Please ensure both gates are firmly re-secured.* Now keep on downhill, on a track which runs under electricity wires and loops down towards a watercourse. When the track forks (**15min**), head left.

In a minute come to the stream bed: cross it, and then cross over another, larger, stream bed lined with plane trees. Follow the narrow track round to the right, to a FENCE. Then take the path along the left-hand side of the fence. Soon (**19min**) cross a stream bed which runs down from the ridge on your left. Keep following the path beside the fence, to pass a first E4 MARKER POLE () and then a SECOND E4 MARKER POLE (**22min**). Your track, still following the fence, widens slightly at this point. One minute later (**23min**) a fenced area is directly in front of you, with a sign, 'Please close the door'. But *do not* go through this gate. Instead, follow the path heading right along the side of

In the Prassanos Gorge

this new fence, passing an E4 MARKER POLE WITH TWO ARROWS. After about 20m/yds, the fence turns sharply left. At this point scramble *carefully* down the steep bank to the watercourse below, taking any

one of the faint sheep trails. Then follow the watercourse to the left, towards the mouth of the gorge. Very soon you will reach the main river bed which has water in it for most of the year. Cross the river at this point and head for the LARGE CONCRETE CYLINDER with an E4 ARROW ahead and slightly to the left, in the middle of the river bed (❷). This is the beginning of the **Prassanos Gorge** (**25min**). *There are no more E4 signs en route.*

Some **33min** into the walk, a wall of the gorge rears up dramatically on your left. At **40min** the river bed swings left (northwest), and proceeds amongst smooth white boulders. Fantastic rock faces are now all round. When you are confronted with a huge rock face ahead, the river bed swings 90° to the left, and you encounter some really big boulders, two of which form a kind of opening through which you pass. There may well be birds of prey hovering over-head here.

Before long (**48min**) the gorge looks impassable: a 2.5m/8ft drop is in front of you. To avoid it, retrace your steps until you find an easy scramble up the right-hand side of the gorge. Scramble up about 20m/yds and look for a goat trail marked by cairns. Follow the trail for 100m/yds or so, until it even-tually meets the river bed further on. This detour takes about 15 minutes. Now just enjoy the splendour of the gorge; unless there has been recent storm damage, there aren't any more sections as awkward as the one just avoided — although there are a few more climbs/drops from boulder to boulder before the way eases out.

The gorge narrows (**1h20min**), and the river bed is gravelly underfoot. You reach the last narrow pass where the gorge is no more than 4m/12ft wide (**1h50min**). Fifteen minutes later (**2h05min**) you will be beyond the main part of the gorge, but still on the river bed. You come to a CONCRETE ROAD BRIDGE across the gorge (**❸**; **2h20min**): walk under the bridge through one of the six circular 'arches' and continue down the gorge. (*From this point on, there is a dirt road on your left. If you are tired, or want a change from walking on boulders, scramble up the bank to this road. It eventually becomes the asphalt road to Missiria.*)

Later you pass some olive groves on the left (**2h30min**). The groves are dotted between factories from here to the mouth of the gorge; this area is becoming quite industrialised.

At the first factory (at time of writing) asphalt comes under foot.

Continue down the river bed until it bends to the right (**3h**). Just after this bend, you'll see an attractive gently arching BRIDGE (**❹**) spanning the river bed and become aware of a faint dirt track/path leading left, out of the river bed (above you, on the bank, there is another factory). Take this track, then turn right on the road. Continue past more factories and a cement works on the right.

Eventually you fork right, to walk under the A90 NATIONAL HIGHWAY and then meet the old main road to Rethimnon in the village of Missiria. Turn left on the road: 150m/yds along, on the right-hand side of the road, there is a bus stop and a public phone box, as well as cafés and tavernas. The BUS STOP (**◯**) is beyond the SIGN FOR **Missiria** (**3h30min**). Alternatively, you can hail a taxi on this road.

View to the Prassanos Gorge from near Prasies

Walk 8: RETHIMNON • CHROMONASTIRI • MYLI

See map page 69
Distance: 11km/6.8mi;
3h35min
Grade: ● moderate, with an
ascent of under 350m/1150ft
Equipment: walking trainers,
sunhat, long socks, picnic, water
Picnic: Profitis Ilias, the pine
wood just afterwards or
Kapadiana spring
Access: 🚌 to Rethimnon bus
station and back (Timetables 1,
2); journey time 1h; then 🚕 taxi
or 🚌 town bus to the kiosk at

the corner of Theotokopoulou
Street on the eastern outskirts of
town, where the walk starts. If it
is very hot it's worth avoiding
the pull out of town by taking
the taxi to either Profitis Ilias
(at the 15min-point) or a bus
or taxi to the Agia Irini
Monastery. Return by 🚌 from
Myli (not in the timetables;
departs 14.55, 16.55, 18.55,
20.55 daily), or 🚕 taxi from
Myli (telephone for one on
arrival), or tack on Walk 9.

This walk takes in a busy seaside town and two old
villages — one of them still without a through road.
And you have the option to extend it through a wonderful
gorge, by following Walk 9 back down to the coast.

Start out east of **Rethimnon**
centre, at a road junction with a
blue road sign on the right to
'ROUSSOSPITI' and a brown sign
to 'AG EIRINI NUNNERY' (later
called 'MONASTERY'). There is a
kiosk on the corner, after which
you will see the street name —
THEOTOKOPOULOU STREET (◉).
Walk straight on up the hill, past
a SCHOOL on the left, ignoring
turnings left and right and going
under the national highway.
You'll soon see the small church
of **Profitis Ilias** perched on a
hill. At the first hairpin bend
after passing under the highway,

there is a solitary house
(**15min**). Walk just to the right
of the house on a bit of rough
track to cut a bend off your
ascent. On the road again,
quickly head off right to the
(fenced-off) church — a lovely
picnic setting, with a splendid
view over Rethimnon.
Go back down to the road, turn
left and, within 80m/yds, take an
asphalted single-lane road that
veers sharp right, above the road
you are on. There is a fresh-
smelling pine wood on your left
— another pretty spot for a
picnic. Ignore any trails through

the pines; keep right. As the asphalt road ends, you encounter three tracks to the left (❶): ignore them all; keep on this right-hand track. Soon the way levels out. Every pace immerses you further in the countryside.

Some 10 minutes from the asphalt, ignore a turning left and keep walking through olive groves and vineyards. A minute later, where a well-concreted track leads up right and a rough track goes left just ahead of you, keep straight ahead on the main track. Shortly after this 'crossroads', your track goes steeply downhill, where it crosses a WATERCOURSE (❷) and goes up the other side, soon passing some fig trees.

Meet a T-junction (**50min**) with a concreted track and turn right. The monastery is high up in front of you, but not yet in sight. In 10 minutes (**1h**), where the main concrete track bends right, ignore a concrete track off left to a house. Walk into and through **Agia Irini** (**1h 10min**). On the far side of the village, turn left downhill on an asphalt road, passing to the left of the **Agia Irini Monastery**.

You will become aware of a church* perched far up on the top of Vrissinas, the mountain in the distance. The summit of Vrissinas, a Minoan peak sanctuary, was excavated in 1972, and samples of the many votive offerings found in rock clefts are now displayed at Rethimnon's Archaeological Museum.

Some **1h20min** en route, take the asphalt road which forks right and is signposted in Greek 'Καπαδιανα (Kapadiana) 2km' (❸). The fork is just before the main part of **Roussospiti**, which you keep to your left. Follow the road and continue on up to the right steeply, levelling out slightly at a junction. Go straight across, veering right; then, at the cross-roads (where there is a block of mail boxes on left), go left on an asphalted road signposted in Greek to ΑΓΙΟΥ ΦΑΝΟΥΡΙΟΥ (❹).

Now, as you gently descend towards Kapadiana, you come to a small BRIDGE at the lowest point on the road (❺; **1h55min**). Set off to the right here is a leafy, cool, open PICNIC AREA with a SPRING. Have a rest in the shade if you like, before continuing. Very shortly past the next bends (left and then right) take the track off to the right, signposted in Greek ΠΡΟΣ

*If you would like to visit the church (which the locals call Agios Pnevma or 'Holy Spirit') another day, you can drive *almost* all the way to the summit from near Kapadiana (see map). Park your car in a grazing area beyond two E4 waymarking poles on the left and follow the E4 path up the west side of the mountain (30 minutes uphill on foot).

Left: Rethimnon's Venetian harbour

ΕΚΛΗΣΕΙΑ' (to the church; (**❻**)'. Ignore all turnings off this track and in a few minutes you will walk past a CHURCH on the left. Just beyond the church, the track forks. Take the right-hand fork (**❼**) and continue down this track as it skirts a hillside to the left and a wooded ravine to the right. Shortly, the track descends to a junction with another track. Continue ahead (left) on this new track (**❽**).

The route opens out (**2h20min**) and you can see Chromonastiri straight ahead. Follow the track round a bend; then, after about three minutes, take the first right turn, along an earthen track. Cross two small concrete BRIDGES. Beyond an orange grove on your left, the track becomes a mostly-cobbled path again and starts climbing towards the village.

Cross over a road (**2h45min**) and walk past houses on a concreted track. In two to three minutes, take a left turn to the newer, unshaded square in **Chromonastiri**, where there are a couple of *cafeneions*. (There is a shady square closer to the village centre.) Head across the square, past a CHURCH on the left and an OBELISK on the right, and turn left on the road beyond it (**2h55min**), to go downhill. Very soon, just after a SHRINE on the right, take the road off to the right. In spring masses of daisies line the route. When you meet the main road again, go left downhill, then follow a wide bend to the right, round the end of a deep verdant ravine filled with chestnut and fig trees.

Ten minutes after joining the road you will see a stone church/shrine (**❾**; **Agios Antonios**; **3h20min**) and steps off right, down into the **Myli Gorge**. Take them and, at the bottom, as you come to an old CHURCH, go down right towards the water channel. There's a spring just beyond the church, should you want to fill your bottle. Follow the path beside, in and over the WATER CHANNEL. When it forks, go left over a concrete bridge (*or, if you are continuing on Walk 9, keep straight ahead here, down the Myli Gorge*). For the main walk, go up the left-hand side of the ravine to explore the enchanting **Agios Ioannis** chapel, built into the rock. Then continue along the WATER CHANNEL to the main road (with BUS STOP, (**❹**), cross over and head up into modern-day **Myli** (**❍**; **3h35min**).

Church in Kato (lower) Myli. (Walk 9)

Walk 9: MYLI GORGE

See photographs on page 67 and opposite

Distance: 4.3km/2.6mi; 1h20min

Grade: ● gorge walk descending 250m/820ft; you must be agile

Equipment: walking trainers, sunhat, picnic, water

Picnic: in the gorge

Access: 🚖 taxi or Chromonastiri 🚌 to Myli (not in the timetables; departs Rethimnon 08.15, 10.15, 12.15, 14.15, 16.15, 18.15). Ask to be dropped below Myli village, at the steps leading down into the gorge. Return by town 🚌 on the coastal road at Perivolia.

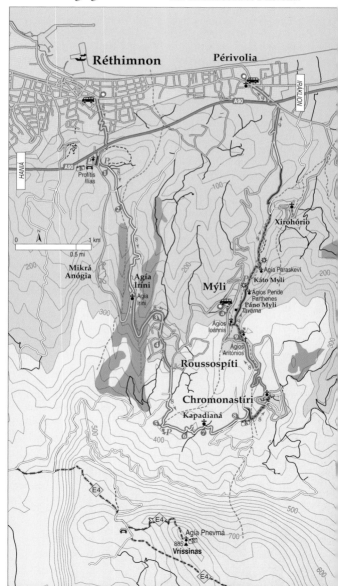

Myli, the name of this wonderfully-cool, shady gorge and the virtually-deserted village beside the stream, derives from the many watermills in the area, which were active in Venetian times.

Start the walk below the modern village of **Myli**, at the STEPS LEADING DOWN TO THE GORGE (**a**). Pass the chapel of **Agios Ioannis**, built into the rock on the right, cross a concrete bridge, and come into **Pano** (upper) **Myli**, where there is a pleasant taverna (with rooms). Here you can pick up an information leaflet about the gorge, its history, flora and fauna. Leave the taverna and take the slightly higher of two paths; it is cobbled and waymarked and heads north towards the sea. Within a couple of minutes you pass the (locked) church of **Agios Pende Parthenes** up on the right. Just after that the route becomes earthen path as it descends to the bottom of the **Myli Gorge** (**15min**), where there are many small waterfalls and ruined mills in the hillsides, once fed by the stone aqueducts that drop from mill to mill.

The path crosses to the other side of the stream at **Kato** (lower) **Myli**, and you look down on the small church of

Agia Paraskevi, on the right. After the path goes under the arch of a ruined building, you can reach the church by crossing the river bed (which might be a rushing torrent). During the walk there are several places to cross on stepping stones, and several chapels to visit. Be sure to leave any stock control gates you find them.

In **1h** you will be out of the main part of the gorge. The path joins a concreted track and crosses the river bed again. Pretty Xirohorio is to the right, but has no public tansport, unfortunately. Ten minutes later you join the Myli/Chromonastiri road: turn right and continue for just under 150m.

When you come to a wide bend to the left, where there is a triangle of flowers and a telegraph pole, walk straight ahead, taking a concreted short-cut to the main road, visible below. You pass a few industrial buildings.

Five minutes downhill will bring you to a crossroads with a main road: turn left and walk downhill. The A90 national highway is over to the right; your route (which you can't see from here) takes you under the highway on a bit of pavement. Then keep left at the Y-fork (a petrol station is to the right) and walk on to a T-junction, where PLATANIA is signposted right and 'BEACH OLD' half-right. You can catch a town bus here in **Perivolia** (**1h20min**): go left to a BUS STOP 50m along (**o**),

Walk 10: GOUVERNETO AND KATHOLIKOU

See photograph on page 42
Distance: 4.3km/2.7mi; 1h30min
Grade: ● moderate-strenuous, with a steep descent/reascent of 260m/850ft; *caution and agility* required beyond Moni Katholikou
Equipment: walking trainers,

sunhat, picnic, water, (swimming things — optional), torch, suitable dress to enter the monastery (see page 25 for opening times).
Picnic: at the 5min-point
Access: 🚌 to Moni Gouverneto (Car tour 4, page 26; 35° 35.075'N, 24° 8.406'E)

The Akrotiri Peninsula, mushrooming out into the sea east of Hania, invites exploration. This walk follows an ancient path, originally traced by a hermit who, in the eleventh century, founded what is considered to be the island's earliest monastery, Moni Katholikou. It's a steep descent, with interesting sites en route.

Start out from the CAR PARK (○) at **Moni Gouverneto**: walk to the left of the walled monastery, then take the stepped, beautifully cobbled path (by a WAR MEMORIAL) leading down the hillside towards the sea. A red arrow on a SHRINE to your left will direct you initially. In **5min** you enjoy some lovely views, especially down over the rocky coast — a good place to picnic.

Further downhill, leave the path and turn right to a cool CAVE (**❶**; **10min**), with a chapel dedicated to **Panagia Arkoudiotissa** at its entrance and a huge, bear-shaped stalagmite in its centre. It is believed that this holy place pre-dates Minoan times.

Continue down, following the clear path which starts to zigzag (**15min**). Just before you reach ruined Moni Katholikou (abandoned on account of repeated pirate raids), you can visit the large CAVE of **Agios Ioannis** (**❷**) on the left; this one contains the grave of the hermit saint in its deepest recess, which you can see by torchlight.

Now descend to **Moni Katholikou** (**25min**), built into the escarpment beside an impressive arched bridge over the narrow gorge. A path heads west from here to Stavros.

Should you decide to scramble down to the river bed, the marginally more passable route is *beyond* the building on the left side of the bridge. It requires caution and agility. Once down, it's 12 minutes to the rocky edge of the sea (**40min**). It's difficult to swim here unless you make your way round to the left, where there is an old quarry slipway (**❸**).

To return, retrace your steps to **Moni Gouverneto** (○; **1h30min**).

Walk 11: RODOPOS • AGIOS IOANNIS GIONIS • RODOPOS

Distance: 18.5km/11.5mi; 5h30min (20.3km/12.6mi if decending to Agios Pavlos)
Grade: ● straightforward but taxing, with ups and downs totalling 550m/1800ft (670m/2200 if visiting Agios Pavlos). The initial descent is steep, and the final climb, while gradual, is long. *Very little shade en route.*
Equipment: walking trainers, sunhat, cover-up protection from the sun, picnic, plenty of water
Picnic: Agios Ioannis Gionis

Access: 🚌 to/from Rodopos; park in the square (35° 33.702'N, 23° 45.311'E). Or 🚐 to Rodopos (not in the timetables, but departs Hania 13.00, 13.20 Mon-Fri); journey time 50min. Or 🚐 to Kolimbari (Timetables 7, 8); journey time 30min, then 🚌 taxi from there to Rodopos (the taxi rank is at the main crossroads). Return with 🚌 taxi from Rodopos to Kolimbari (telephone from the *cafeneion* in the village square), then 🚐 to Hania (Timetables 7, 8).

One can't fail to notice the Rodopou Peninsula on the map of Crete, jutting out into the sea with the Gramvousa Peninsula — rather like a rabbit's ears. The peninsulas invite exploration. This walk starts and finishes in the very pleasant square in Rodopos village; all the locals collect here to pass the time of day and watch the world go by. You will be enveloped in quietness and a miles-away-from-it-all feeling on this peninsula. The walk is well waymarked, and few trees obscure the route. The few trees, however, offer very little shade, so this is *not* a hike for high summer. Getting into the church of Agios Ioannis Gionis is not an essential part of the walk but, if you wish to do so, ask for the key in Rodopos.

The bus turns round in the village square at **Rodopos** (◐). To **start the walk**, leave the square on your right and take the road which leads out north past a BUST (also on the right), in a corner of the square. The road takes you past a large CHURCH on the right — a good landmark when you return to the village from a different direction, at the end of the walk. Two to three minutes later, near the edge of Rodopos, pass another much smaller and very pretty CHURCH tucked back on the right. Keep straight on. Five minutes' walking will take

you out of the village. Ten minutes later (**15min**), the road starts to bend. After the first big hairpin bend to the left, look for a path going uphill to the right, with a stone wall on its left-hand side: it cuts some loops off the road. When you meet the road again, head right. Eventually tarmac gives way to gravel, as you continue in the same northerly direction. At **45min** the gravel road passes a CONCRETE PILLAR (❶). Ignore the track heading off right beyond it; go straight ahead. Ten minutes later the sea is in sight behind you and to your right.

Some 25 minutes from Agios Ioannis Gionis, you look down to the sea and another church, Agios Pavlos. (This photograph was taken before the new gravel road to the chapel was built.)

Then these views are lost, as the route bends left and inland. After **1h** walking a track peels off left; continue on the gravel road you have been following and in another five minutes the sea will come into sight again over to the right. Soon TWO CISTERNS (❷; **1h15min**) are ahead to the left and there is a sign in Greek indicating that the way to Agios Ioannis Gionis is to the right. The sign is for *vehicles*. Head off *left* beside the cisterns, on a smaller track (more like a goats' trail — or like a stream bed after wet weather). One or two minutes past the cisterns, cross a track and continue straight on. A couple of minutes later curve round to the right. Continue round to the right and then, where the track forks a minute later, keep left uphill.

The track soon runs out (**1h25min**), in an open area where there is a building set down to the left. Walk straight ahead in the direction you have been heading. Then go right and find a waymark indicating a path leading to a low wall on which a METAL SHRINE (❸) is bolted. Look over the wall and you will see the gravel road you were originally following continuing downhill — to the dilapidated but attractively-sited church of Agios Ioannis Gionis far below. Secluded by trees and surrounded by open grazing land, the church is protected from the sea beyond by a ridge. To the left, the end of the Gramvousa Peninsula (photograph page 17) is visible, reaching out into the sea. Take the footpath to the left of the low wall and wind slowly downhill. Within a couple of turns you pass a MINIATURE CHURCH perched on a rock. Some 35 minutes of careful walking on the loose earth-and-rubble path will bring you to the flat area around **Agios Ioannis Gionis** (❹; **2h15min**). To visit the church, cross the open ground in front of it. There are two concrete WCs to the left of it. The church is an obvious place to rest and picnic, in the welcome shade of a plane tree.

Anyone and everyone who is called Ioannis can come here on one particular day in the year to be baptised … that's a lot of Johns!

From here go back to the SHRINE where the footpath ended and follow the road south, past some olive groves and vineyards. Eventually Kastelli and the Kissamos Gulf come into view. Some 25 minutes from the church (**2h40min**) you look down to another church by the sea, **Agios Pavlos** (**❹**). Where the gravel road makes a hairpin down to the church, keep straight ahead. (Or allow an extra couple of kilometres and 120m/400ft of descent and reascent if you go down to see the church.)

Continue on across the hillside, parallel with the sea, on a cairned and occasionally waymarked path. Some 1h20min from Agios Ioannis Gionis (**3h35min**) a few trees near a ravine provide rare and welcome shade. Below, the vivid blue sea curls tantalisingly up onto the rocky coastline. A patch of small carob trees, again by a ravine, offers a further brief shady interlude. Ten to 15 minutes beyond here the path curls uphill (**3h45min**). Look ahead, across the hillside, and you will see your way back to Rodopos. A 30-minute climb lies ahead; watch for the sporadic waymarking as you cross the hillside.

At the top of the climb there are TROUGHS and a container used as a SHEPHERDS' HUT (**❺**) — and more gravel road. It's quite nice to be on the flat! Walk right on the gravel, heading south, back to Rodopos. Some 45 minutes

from getting onto this road and leaving the container shed, having passed pasture on the left, then animal pens and a stock shed on the right, and finally a vineyard on the left, Rodopos will be in view, with its easily-recognisable church. Stay on the gravel road and, when it becomes surfaced, go right. Then take the first left turn, up to the village square in **Rodopos** (**❍**; **5h30min**).

Mullein
(Verbascum thapsiforme)

Spiny acanthus
(Acanthus spinosus)

Thorny burnet
(Sarcopoterium spinosum)

Cretan ebony
(Ebenus cretica)

Jerusalem sage
(Phlomis fruticosa)

Shrub tobacco
(Nicotiana glauca)

Walk 12: A CIRCUIT FROM KOLIMBARI VIA MONI GONIA

Distance: 12km/7.5mi; 2h30min

Grade: ● a straightforward walk on roads and tracks, with an ascent/descent of about 250m/ 800ft overall

Equipment: walking trainers, sunhat, picnic, water, suitable clothing for a visit to the monastery (trousers for men and longish skirts for women).

Note: Moni Gonia is open 08.00-

12.00 and 16.00-19.00 daily except Saturday.

Picnic: at Kolimbari port or Moni Gonia

Access: 🚗 or 🚐 to/from Kolimbari (Timetables 7, 8) or one of the frequent buses running between Kastelli-Kissamos and Hania. Drivers can park near the old port shown opposite (**❶**; 35° 32.766'N, 23° 46.710'E).

This short but interesting foray into the Cretan countryside combines the quiet attraction of hillside and coastal villages with an opportunity to visit a peaceful seaside monastery. Starting in Kolimbari, a relaxed backwater just off the national highway, within easy reach of Hania, the walk goes through the very attractive villages of Afrata and Astratigos, past and through fields, down into a valley and up again, before returning to the sea at Kolimbari.

Start the walk in **Kolimbari**: whether on foot from the bus or in your car, follow the sign 'AFRATA 5KM' from the main crossroads (**O**). This road first passes Kolimbari's PORT (**❶**), where it is most convenient to leave your car.

You then pass the 17th-century Venetian fortress monastery, **Moni Gonia** (**15min**). It was an important centre for Cretan Resistance fighters during the Second World War. (When we wrote the first editions of this book, a key figure in the Resistance was running a hotel at the main crossroads under the his wartime code name, Rosmarie.)

Continue along the road as it climbs the cliff to Afrata. Compensating for the asphalt there are beautiful sea views as you climb, then the route turns inland through olive groves and

vineyards. In **Afrata** (**1h**) walk past the church to a small square with two *cafeneions,* a nice place to relax. Then follow signposting to the left for 'ASTRATIGOS 2KM', heading up beside a ravine which you will cross later.

Arriving in **Astratigos** (**1h25min**), walk past a church on your left. At the end of the village you approach the back of a road sign, on your right. About 20m/yds after passing this sign, take the GRAVEL TRACK (**❷**) heading obliquely left and gently downhill. Follow this track until you reach a CONCRETED SECTION (**❸**) at a junction. Turn left, downhill — and slightly back on yourself. The track now meanders to the valley floor through olive groves, then begins to rise out of the valley on the other side. At the first Y-fork after crossing the valley floor (**❹**), go left. Under

The harbour at Kolimbari. Take a break here at Mylos, a pleasant café in a converted mill by the water's edge, opposite the bakery/ confectioners. Moni Gonia is visible in the background.

200m/yds further on, at the top of the rise — with lovely views to the sea — turn right at a T-junction (**1h45min**). Stay on this main track, ignoring a turning left, until you come to a cross tracks, some 10 minutes later, where there is a large SHRINE on the left (**⑤**). Go straight across, descending on concrete. Six minutes later, in amongst a rather unsightly band of houses, the track becomes road just before a junction. This is **Grimbiliana**, the heart of which is an attractive old village.

Take the first turning left; the road curves round to the right and comes to a junction with another road. Turn left and head down towards the sea (**⑥**). When the road forks between the houses of **Kolimbari** (**⑦**; **2h20min**), almost at sea level, keep right, into the middle of the village. Before heading right, back to the bus stop at the start of the village, turn left and, after 150m/yds, turn down to the

HARBOUR (**①**) to pick up your car. If you came by bus, retrace your steps to the MAIN CROSS-ROADS (**〇**) and the BUS STOP (**2h30min**).

Walk 13: FROM SIRIKARI TO POLIRINIA

See photograph on page 10
Distance: 7km/4.3mi; 2h20min
Grade: ● straightforward; an
easy gorge walk with a steep
initial descent of about 300m/
1000ft, then an easy gorge walk
and a gentle ascent of 200m/
650ft (add another 120m/390ft
if you climb to the acropolis)
Equipment: walking trainers,
sunhat, picnic, water
Picnic: at the rest area in the
gorge or below Polirinia
Access: 🚌 to Kastelli-Kissamos
(Timetable 8); journey time
45min. Change to Sirikari 🚌
(not in the timetables, but
departs Mondays and Fridays
only at 14.00 (enquire locally);
journey time 1h. Return with
🚗 taxi from Polirinia to Kastelli

(best to organise this before you
leave Kastelli). Then 🚌 from
Kastelli (Timetable 8).
Alternative walk: ● Sirikari to
Kastelli-Kissamos (12.5km/
7.6mi; 3h30min). Grade/equip-
ment/ access as main walk.
From the vine-covered taverna
in **Polirinia** (**4**), retrace your
steps out of the village. After
the last building on the left,
descend a path left, to the road.
Turn left on the road but,
almost immediately, turn right
on a track. Follow this all the
way to Kastelli. It becomes
asphalted halfway along and
eventually brings you into
Kastelli beside a supermarket .
Turn left for the BUS STATION.

The gorge leading to Polirinia is wide, pretty and
wonderfully peaceful — filled with bright yellow
Jerusalem sage in spring and crisp pink and white oleander
in summer. And a bonus to this delightful walk is a visit
to Kastelli, a very pleasant town where the local people
are particularly charming and helpful. Taking a morning
bus from Hania gives you time to wander round Kastelli,
before catching your onward bus to Sirikari — a journey
affording splendid views, as you wind into the heart of the
countryside.

Get off the bus where it turns
round just beyond **Sirikari**, by a
solitary CHURCH (**O**). **Start out**
by taking the path at the right of
an INFORMATION BOARD in the
church car park. You pass
through a waymarked STOCK
CONTROL GATE almost at once
and descend quite dteeply
towards the gorge. When you
meet a concrete track (**5min**)
follow it to the right. After
about 50m/yds, the path
becomes a track at an OLD
FARMSTEAD. Weave between
the buildings and bear right
where the path divides.

Keep on the waymarked path
along the right-hand side of
the valley. The river bed is
lined with leafy plane trees.
Soon the route is at the
beginning of the GORGE, and
the air is light and fresh. Keep
to the path on the right-hand
side of the river bed. About
halfway along, you will pass
some well-placed rustic PICNIC
TABLES (**1**), a good place for a
break.
By **1h25min** the path has taken
you well up the right-hand side
of the gorge, and the landscape
has opened up. Soon, another

valley meets this one from the right, and the village of Polirinia can be seen ahead in the distance, its church set on the heights. Cross a pretty, old cobbled VENETIAN BRIDGE (**❷**; **1h35min**), then continue parallel with the river bed, now on your right, past some fencing. The path soon widens into a track, passing a concrete PUMP HOUSE (**❸**) on the left. Walk uphill to and through a STOCK CONTROL FENCE and turn right downhill, following the track until it merges with a road coming from the right (**1h50min**). Follow this road uphill. Soon you pass the first houses of Polirinia. This is another pleasant setting for a countryside picnic (see photograph on page 10). Although there are short-cut paths up through the houses, from here the most straightforward route into the village is via the road — follow it to the left uphill (keeping right at a Y-fork); then, where it meets the main road Kastelli/Polirinia road, turn sharp right in a tight hairpin bend and follow it round into **Polirinia** (**2h20min**). You emerge at a small open area with a VINE-COVERED TAVERNA (**❹**). A taxi, or friends, could meet you here.

Otherwise, if you are still feeling energetic, we urge you to carry on with the Alternative walk to Kastelli, a very pleasant 5.5km-long downhill stroll through olive groves, with frequent views of the coast below.

Before leaving Polirinia, take time to walk east through the village, to explore the 'ANCIENT FORTIFICATION TOWER' and

AQUEDUCT (there's a place to fill water bottles too). From the CAFENEION in another small open area, in the centre of the village, you could climb the steep steps up to the CHURCH AND CEMETERY (**❺**). From there a path winds up to the right, rounding the ACROPOLIS HILL. It's worth making the effort — you will have a splendid view from the top. And there is the handy Acropolis Taverna (**❻**) just a couple of hundred metres further west along the ridge — another place where a taxi or friends could collect you.

Distance: 11.4km/7mi; 3h20min

Grade: ● easy-moderate, with an initial ascent of about 250m/800ft, followed by a descent (sometimes a scramble) of 450m/1500ft

Equipment: walking trainers, sunhat, picnic, water

Picnic: Katsomatados, near the start of the walk

Access: Elafonisi 🚐 to Katsomatados (not in the timetables, but departs 09.00 daily; journey time 1h10min. Or 🚐 to Kastelli-Kissamos (Timetable 8); journey time 45min, then 🚐 to Katsomatados (not in the timetables, departs 10.00);

journey time 20min. Or by 🚗: park in Katsomatados (35° 24.328'N, 23° 40.933'E). Return on 🚐 from Voulgaro to Kastelli (not in the timetables, departs 17.10 daily); journey time 10min, then 🚐 to Hania (Timetable 8). Do *not* rely on the return Elafonisi bus, since it may well be full and not stop. Alternatively, if you travelled by car to Katsomatados, take a 🚕 taxi from Voulgaro back to Katsomatados, to pick up your car (enquire about taxis at the first *cafeneion* you come to in Voulgaro, on the right-hand side of the road).

A fine wedge of lovely and varied countryside, is covered in this walk. We take you through a gorge, along a pretty chestnut tree-lined valley, into some sweeping open countryside, and finally down a ravine well used by grazing flocks of sheep and goats. There's some scrambling en route, but for the most part the walk is on well-defined track.

If you take a taxi from Kastelli-Kissamos, the driver will stop for you to look down into the Topolia Gorge before dropping you on the outskirts of Katsomatados; otherwise you can see the gorge walls quite well from the bus. If travelling by bus, ask to be dropped off about 350m/yds beyond the approach sign for the village of Katsomatados. (The sign says 'Koutsoumatados', but the villagers are adamant that this is a newfangled and ugly name, so we have obliged them.) Here, not far past the OASIS TAVERNA (○), a concrete track leads down into the village (signposted: 'SQUARE, TAVERNA, PARKING').

Start the walk by taking this track, going over a BRIDGE and

past the large taverna called 'Hiker' (with rooms to rent), on the left. Go straight ahead, over a water channel, and onto a track (concreted initially). Pass a pretty CHURCH on the left and continue along the very pleasant, shady track. Plane trees and chestnuts, olives and oleander keep everything cool, growing along the watercourse on the left. Anywhere along here is pleasant for picnicking. You are in the valley shown in the centre of the photograph opposite, a lush green setting.

Ignore first a right and then a left fork (the latter crossing over the stream bed); keep the stream bed on your left now. At **15min** you come to a stock control gate: leave it as you find it. The track starts to climb and, five minutes later, is concreted for about 40m/yds. At a junction (**20min**) follow the track as it bends sharply to the left uphill (**❶**).

Walk out of the shade as the track becomes much wider, leading through open countryside, with gentle green hills all round. Pass a STONE SHELTER to the left and walk straight ahead on a track dotted with wooden and/or metal FEEDING TROUGHS. It's a 30-minute climb to the top, from where there are wonderful views, as you can see in the photograph on page 83. Twenty minutes from the troughs you come to an intersection where the choice is a gradual right bend going downhill or a SHARP RIGHT BEND going uphill (**❷**): follow the latter. At the SADDLE, soon ignore the two tracks going off left and right; go straight ahead through a stock control gate (**❸**; signposted in Greek to AG ATHANASIOS; **50min**). Keep on the track as it bends round to the left, ignoring a track going off sharply to the right (it leads down to Sasalos; Walk 15). A few minutes along you can see the village of Sasalos below on the right.

Eight minutes past the view over Sasalos, your track (which *may be* signposted to Agios Athanasios) forks downhill to the left (**4**); ignore another track which goes straight ahead and forks. Pass between vineyards and some olive trees on the right. In five minutes you will be facing a mesh fence blocking the path to the stream bed directly in front. Make your way to the

church of **Agios Athanasios** on the far bank. From here a well-defined path runs diagonally back to the stream bed. Leave via the gated fence on the far side of the church.

Once in the stream bed (**1h15min**), head north-northeast along it; a rough path leads you beside, in and over the dry watercourse. Goats and sheep wander about and sit in the shade, close to the piped water running along the route. The stream bed becomes a ravine

We've climbed high enough now to look back to the village of Katsomatados, seen below in the valley. Walk 15 enjoys this same view on the descent to Katsomatados and Topolia. Picnic 14 is set below, in the valley.

a bit further on, where the animals shelter from the sun. Walking here in spring and early summer you'll find a mass of pungent dragon lilies standing sentry, together with thick Jerusalem sage. At **1h30min** come to a point where you can see through high, sloping rock walls to the countryside beyond. The route then starts to descend steeply, as the stream bed becomes a ravine. It's necessary to scramble in places. Keep to the left-hand side. Five minutes later, at the narrowest point, a stock control fence might bar the way: negotiate it and continue downhill, picking your own route. Within 10 minutes you emerge on a TRACK (**5**) that crosses the watercourse: turn left.

In early summer you will be surrounded by bright yellow broom; in autumn the yellows and golds of vineyards lend mellow overtones to the landscape. Soon, beyond another stock control gate, keep on the main track, ignoring any turning

to the left or right. After about 30 minutes, the track — more of a dirt road by now — becomes asphalted, and you meet a fork: walk downhill to the right. Within a few minutes you will pass the first houses of **Mouri**, a very small village. Before long, pass an old *cafeneion* on the right (**2h25min**), shaded by vines and mulberries. Keep ahead on the asphalt road, passing a CHURCH on your left as you leave Mouri. Twenty minutes from the *cafeneion*, the road winds down into the tiny hamlet of **Katohori**, looping round a concrete, red-tiled CHURCH en route. Voulgaro can be seen across the valley and, a bit further on, the village of Topolia comes into view, with the narrow gorge leading to Katsomatados to its left. The road eventually passes a small road off south to Latziana (**6**), then crosses the river bed. When you meet the main road, turn right into **Voulgaro** (**O**; **3h20min**) and ask at the nearest *cafeneion*, about buses or taxis.

Walk 15: SASALOS • KATSOMATADOS • TOPOLIA

See also photograph page 83
Distance: 9km/5.5mi; 2h15min
Grade: ● quite easy, with ascents of 300m/1000ft and descents of 350m/1150ft overall
Equipment: walking trainers, sunhat, picnic, water; *small torch*
Picnic: Katsomatados
Access: 🚌 to Kastelli-Kissamos (Timetable 8); journey time 45min; then 🚌 to Sasalos (not in the timetables, departs 14.00 Tuesdays and Fridays *only;* enquire locally); journey time approximately 1h. Or Kastelli 🚕

taxi to Sasalos. Return on 🚌 from Topolia to Kastelli (not in the timetables, departs about 16.45 daily); journey time 30min; or 🚕 taxi to Kastelli. Then 🚌 to Hania (Timetable 8); journey 45min
Short walk: Sasalos — Katsomatados (5km/3mi; 1h35min). ● Follow the main walk to Katsomatados and either hail a 🚕 taxi on the main road outside the village or call for one from one of the *cafeneions* on the main road.

Taking a straightforward route from Sasalos to Topolia, this walk makes a delightful afternoon's ramble. The countryside stays green throughout the summer, oleanders cover the hillsides, and leafy chestnut trees line and shade the country track for part of the way. Give yourselves plenty of time to wander round Kastelli-Kissamos before taking the onward bus to Sasalos.

No matter where the bus stops, **start out** by walking on into **Sasalos** (⦿), passing a road off left signposted to 'FLORIA'. Then go right, over a BRIDGE and, just past a building on the right, turn right on an earthen track. Walk past an old barn-like building set back from the road and head towards a CHURCH (❶). At the church, turn right along the watercourse and follow the track through the trees. When you meet a road coming from the village, join it and head left uphill. In five minutes, the road bends right into the hamlet of Papadiana (❷). Go left here; the tarmac gives way immediately to a concrete and gravel track. Follow this uphill, ignoring any turn-offs.
Eventually, the track levels out (**40min**). You can see the track to Voulgaro (Walk 14) ahead, making a long bend to the right. Look for a short, steep stretch of
84

track heading sharply back to the left and follow it uphill. Go through the stock control gate at the TOP OF THE RIDGE (❸) and you will find yourself looking down over the fertile hills spreading out ahead into the distance (photograph page 83). Three tracks lead off from here: take the middle one; it bends down to a valley which leads to Katsomatados.
A few minutes later, at another fork, head left on the track that goes down towards the bottom of the valley. Some 25 minutes from the top of the ridge, beyond some FEEDING TROUGHS and a stone ANIMAL SHELTER on the right, the track enters the tree line. Ignore a footpath signed to 'Kastanodasos' (an old chestnut wood) and follow the track as it turns down to the right and crosses the stream. Continue straight downhill, in the shade of leafy chestnuts.

Just beyond a very pretty CHURCH on the right and then a large taverna called 'Hiker', you come into **Katsomatados** (**1h30min**). Continue straight ahead. Cross the BRIDGE over the river bed and bend left with the concrete track, up onto the main asphalt road. Turn right here and walk towards Topolia, 40 minutes away. Some 350m/yds from the junction there's a pleasant taverna on the right (④) called OASIS at time of writing. *(The Short walk ends here; either wait for a taxi to pass or telephone for one.)*

The main walk keeps along the road; soon you see a tunnel cutting into the wall of the **Topolia Gorge**. A few minutes before the tunnel entrance, a sign indicates AGIA SOPHIA (⑤; Αγ Σοφια). This tiny church, built inside a cave with stalactites and stalagmites, is just a 10-minute climb off the road (a star at the top of the church, just visible at the mouth of the cave, can be seen from the road. Having made the effort to climb up ... or not, continue along the main road, negotiating the 150

Agia Sophia cave chapel

metre-long TUNNEL carefully and waving your torch so any motorists know you are there. The Topolia Gorge runs deep to the right of the road. About 200m/yds from the tunnel exit you can admire the view from a small cantina overlooking the gorge.

When you arrive at **Topolia** (**2h15min**) hail a passing taxi. There are usually taxis parked somewhere on the main road in this top part of the village. Or, if you started the walk early (perhaps had a lift), you may be in time for the 15.30 bus. There's a BUS STOP ahead, just before the road hairpins to the right, signposted to 'HANIA 40KM' (⓪).

85

Walk 16: THE AGIA IRINI GORGE

Distance: 12km/7.4mi;
3h30min
Grade: ● straightforward gorge
walk descending about 600m/
2000ft; waymarked. Some short
steep sections require agility.
Plenty of shade except for the
final 2.5km along the road to
Sougia (this can be avoided from
May-October, when a bus leaves
for Sougia from the car park at
the end of the gorge).
Equipment: walking trainers,
sunhat, picnic, water, swimming
things

Picnic: at the gorge rest areas,
with tables, fountains, WCs
Access: Sougia 🚌 (Timetable
6); ask to get off at the Irini
Gorge ('fah-**rah**-gee') itself, or at
Agia Irini (then walk south
downhill for 10min to the gorge)
or at Epanohori (then walk 7min
north uphill to the gorge);
journey time 1h15min. Return
on 🚌 from Sougia (Timetable
6); journey time 1h30min
Note: there is a small fee to enter
the gorge.

The Agia Irini Gorge has been made easily passable by
mechanics and man, perhaps to take some pressure off
the Samaria Gorge — and perhaps to make another tourist
haunt! Although there are seating areas and drinking water
is available, the gorge is still very much in its natural state.
Although not as dramatic as Samaria, Irini makes a good
walk most of the year, and Sougia is a pleasant, somewhat
sleepy, backwater at which to end up and have a swim
before the return. You could even stay overnight there,
walk via Lisos to Paleohora the next day (Walk 17) or even
carry on from Paleohora to Elafonisi (Walk 18) and get a
bus back to Hania from there.

Start the walk on the road to
Sougia, by the SIGNBOARD (**○**)
for the gorge; follow the track
down to a taverna (with
parking), then the ticket kiosk
(with WC). Now the stream bed
starts on your left. Pines scent
the air, and chestnut trees
provide leafy cover as you
approach the **Agia Irini Gorge**.
In seven minutes the track
crosses the stream bed and
before long becomes a path, as it
rises above the stream bed again.
From now on it is straightforward waymarked walking, with
several REST AREAS (**❶-❹**) and
other 'unofficial' places to picnic
surrounded by massive rockfalls
and grandiose scenery.
By **2h30min** you will be aware

that the gorge is ending, as you
look ahead to hillsides. When
there are olive groves on either
side of you (**2h40min**), the
waymarked route heads uphill,
out of the river bed (**❺**). Turn
left on an asphalt road just
beyond a SNACK BAR. Following
the river bed on your right, you
eventually come to a large car
park. Up to the left is a CHURCH,
and down to the right an old
Venetian BRIDGE (**❻**), in the
middle of the river bed.
Continue downhill, join another
road, and turn right over a
BRIDGE (**❼**; just over **3h**). Soon
the road rises to the main Sougia
road: turn left and walk the last
2.5km to **Sougia** (**○**;
3h30min).

In the Agia Irini Gorge

HANIA

Agía Iríni

Epanohóri

Tavérna
Ticket kiosk

962

E4

16

WC

E4

WC

16

Agía Iríni Gorge

0   1 km

0.5 mi

E4

Moní

E4

Konstogérako

E4

Livadás

E4   E4

Ochro
807

16

E4

E4

Soúgia

17
88-89

Walk 17: SOUGIA • LISOS • PALEOHORA

Map continues on pages 90-91
Distance: 15km/9.3mi; 4h45min

Grade: ● moderate-strenuous, with ups and downs of 400m/ 1300ft overall; E4 waymarked

Equipment: walking trainers, sunhat, long socks/trousers, picnic, ample water

Picnic: in the Lisos Gorge

Access: 🚌 to Sougia (Timetable 6); journey time 1h30min. Return on 🚌 from Paleohora (Timetable 5); journey time 2h

Short walk: Sougia — Lisos — Sougia (8km/5mi; 2h30min).

● Moderate climb and descent of 150m/500ft; equipment as main walk. 🚌 to/from Sougia (Timetable 6); journey time 1h30min. Or 🚗 (35° 14.828'N, 23° 48.423'E).

Alternative walk: Sougia circuit (6.6km/4mi; 2h15min).
● Grade/equipment/access as *Short walk* (ups/downs of 250m/ 820ft). Follow the main walk for 30 minutes, then *leave* the E4 and refer to the map. *Orientation skills* needed from leaving the gorge until you join the track; *watch carefully* for the sparse red dot and cairn waymarking.

The bus ride to Sougia, where this walk starts, is through a picturesque wooded valley and tree-clad hillsides — the western foothills of the White Mountains — glorious in autumn colours. The bus follows the Agia Irini Gorge (Walk 16) and river bed down to the Libyan Sea. This sea is ever in view throughout the walk, which parallels the coast. The first stage takes us through an exceedingly pretty gorge, then uphill, over, and down to the ancient Roman site at Lisos, set back from the sheltered bay of Agios Kyrkos. The second pull brings us up and across a large, flat-topped headland, before we head back down to the sea and along a length of coast, punctuated by bays, stretching all the way to Paleohora.

The bus will drop you beside a sweep of shingle beach in **Sougia**. Facing the sea, **start off** by heading right (west) from the BUS STOP/CAR PARKS (⬤). Keep round to the right when the road divides at Sougia's small HARBOUR. A rock face rears up in front of you, and a sign points

you in the direction of LISOS. The path is E4 waymarked and leads into the very pretty gorge shown opposite, thick with brilliant pink oleander in late spring and summer. Choose your picnic spot — under carobs, olives or pines, in the gorge or beside it.

Just **25min** into the walk, the smooth gorge walls tower up above you. Five minutes later, be sure to follow the E4 path up to the left, *leaving* the gorge (**❶**; **30min**). *(The Alternative walk keeps straight on here.)* Some **50min** into the walk you will see Lisos below you, set back from its lovely sheltered bay. The path twists downhill; you pass the mouth of a CAVE (**1h**) up to the right. **Lisos** is reached in about **1h15min**. If the site isn't open, look for the keeper, who can usually be found in his nearby house that doubles up as a REFRESHMENT HUT (or you can open the 'GATE' in the fencing; **❶**). *(The Short walk returns from here to Sougia.)*

From here follow waymarking to the west of the keeper's house, just above a THRESHING FLOOR. Where a DIRT ROAD (**❷**) cuts across your route, cross over, initially on a track.

In under **2h** you should be well within sight of the south coast and your destination. There are some lovely coves in which to swim and enjoy the solitude. By **3h35min** you come upon a long sweep of beach, no doubt dotted with holidaymakers getting an all-over tan. This is south of Anidri, and there is a welcoming TAVERNA as well. Just over an

hour later you will be in **Paleohora** (**4h45min**). You pass the CEMETERY on your right as you come in: 200m/yds past its gate, turn right. Then take the second left, onto the main street. The BUS STOP (**❍**; blue sign) is just ahead to your left, outside a café.

The gorge at Sougia (top) and the keeper's house at Lisos

Walk 18: FROM PALEOHORA (KRIOS BEACH) TO ELAFONISI

See also photograph pages 18-19

Distance: 9.5km/5.9mi; 3h30min

Grade: ●: moderate, with ups and downs of about 300m/ 1000ft overall, but you must be sure-footed and agile, with a head for heights (possibility of vertigo). E4 waymarked

Equipment walking trainers, sunhat, picnic, ample water

Picnic: anywhere en route, but little shade except at Elafonisi

Access: 🚌 to Paleohora (Timetable 5); journey time 2h (or walk from Sougia; Walk 17); then 🚕 taxi to Krios Beach (7km). Return on 🚌 from Elafonisi at 16.00 or 🚌 from Moni Chrisoskalitsas at 18.00 (not in the timetables; *in high summer only*). Or ⛴ back to Paleohora; departs 16.00, 18.00 *in high summer only*

This is a lovely coastal walk, with the sound of the sea accompanying you all the way. Paleohora is a pleasant place to stay — or spend the night if you've walked from Sougia (Walk 17). It has a good bookshop and several

An E4 waymarking pole marks the start of the walk at Krios Beach.

tavernas and café-bars where walkers congregate. From Elafonisi, you could walk 5km to Moni Chrisoskalitisas (shown in the photograph on page 18), visit it, then catch the later (high summer only) bus to Hania from there.

The taxi will drop you by a CANTINA (○) at the edge of **Krios Beach**. Leaving the cantina on your right (and *ignoring* two tracks to a chapel almost directly above), **start out** by heading west across the beach towards the headland, where you clamber over a small rock outcrop by the first E4 waymark post. Then take the rocky path up the hillside — marked with yellow and some old red waymarks.

Some **10min** along, the path rises to a TRACK (❶) at the top of the first headland. Looking back beyond the beach from here, there's the sad sight of acres of plastic greenhouses — all too common along the south coast of Crete — and an unsightly contrast to the lovely sea. As the Elafonisi Peninsula comes into view in the distance, this track forks repeatedly. Keep heading in the same direction, then take the cairned fork that leads down into a rocky cove (❷).

At **1h** the path crosses quite loose scree, and there is no protection from the drops down to the sea — a vertiginous

section. Ten minutes later, having crossed another ridge, the chapel of **Agios Ioannis** (❸) comes into sight. Outside it, there is a huge, inviting bell to ring; there is also a SIGNPOSTED SPRING 50m/yds away.

If you find it hard to spot the next E4 sign, look for a cairn or old red waymark. Another vertiginous section is encountered at **1h40min**. Five minutes later the route *seems* to head uphill, away from the edge of the cliff, but walk to the edge: you may be alarmed to see an E4 sign *below* you. There is a way down! It requires some ten minutes' careful scrambling down onto a beach. Cairns and red waymarks mark the way across the beach.

Waymarking from here on is sporadic, but your direction is clear. If you're taking the BOAT back to Paleohora, you will see it moored, on its own, off the rocks to your left; a small sign indicates departure times.

Beyond are the **Elafonisi** beaches shown on pages 18-19 and cantinas. The Hania BUS leaves from behind the last cantina you reach (**3h30min**).

Walk 19: XILOSKALA • LINOSELI COL • GINGILOS • XILOSKALA

See also top photograph page 98

Distance: 9.2km/5.7mi; 5-6h (14.8km/7h including Volakias)

Grade: ●∷ very strenuous climb and descent of 1000m/ 3300ft overall (1250m including Volakias); you must be sure-footed with a head for heights *(danger of vertigo)*; little shade en route. E4 waymarking initially

Equipment: walking boots, windproof, sunhat, sun protection, picnic, ample water

Picnic: best shade is at the start

Access: 🚌 to/from Omalos (Timetable 3); journey time about 45min (Xiloskala is the last stop, at the top of the Samaria Gorge). In the summer season (May to October) there are more buses returning than are shown in the timetables. Or 🚗 (35° 18.495'N, 23° 55.091'E).

Shorter walk: Xiloskala — Afhenas Col — Xiloskala (7.4km/4.6mi; 3h30min); equipment, access/return as main walk. Grade: ● half the climb and descent (500m/1650ft). Follow the main walk for 1h40min and return the same way. Or go only as far as the Linoseli spring.

By climbing Gingilos you can totally immerse yourself in the deep solitude, silence, echoes and majesty characteristic of high mountain walks. Gingilos is a magnificent and awesome mass, towering to one side of the Samaria Gorge. Wild rock formations, a massive band of scree, echoing stone walls, wild flowers clinging perilously to ledges, contorted, windswept trees, and breathtaking views are just some of this walk's delights.

Walking to the Afhenas Col (the Shorter walk) will probably be more than enough of an experience for some of you, while for others — intrepid types — you can clamber to the top of Volakias. The main walk is easier than it looks when you stand and contemplate the mountain; at 1974m/6475ft (you'll see differing heights on different maps), Gingilos may not be the highest peak on Crete, but it's certainly one of the most inspiring.

The bus turns round at the **Xiloskala** CAR PARK (⊙), the top of the walk down into the Samaria Gorge (Walk 21; Walk 20 also begins here). Facing the wooden railings at the top of the *xiloskala* (Greek for 'wooden staircase'), look right, up

towards a TAVERNA perched on the hillside, off the road. Our hike starts behind it. **Set off** up the path indicated by an E4 sign, passing the taverna. The path, initially with wooden railings, climbs steeply, so you gain height rapidly. Occasional trees at the side of the path give shade for pauses — and an early picnic break (there is very little shade further on).

By the time the path flattens out you are heading well away from the Omalos, which is fast receding behind you. Looking back from here gives you an excellent view of the refuge high up at Kallergi, on the far side of the Samaria Gorge (see photograph on page 98). Notice two paths in particular: one in the foreground comes down to

Dramatic rock formations characterise this exhilarating hike as here at the Xepitiras Arch.

Xiloskala (Walk 20); the other, in the middle distance (to the right of Kallergi) leads through the conservation area into the Samaria Gorge (Walk 21). Where the path begins to run high — and there is a fair drop to the left side (❶; **45min**) vertigo sufferers may feel anxious.

Our path now takes us under the huge **Xeptiras Arch** (❷; **50min**); Cretan ebony hangs gracefully from this rock arch, and you cannot fail to feel as though you're in the very heart of the mountains here. There are massive, dramatic rock faces, peaks, boulders and formations all around, as the photograph above shows.

At **1h15min** into the walk you round a very large overhanging rock on the right; you will notice

a CAVE SHELTER beneath it. Five minutes later, the route leads to the **Linoseli Spring** (❸), where there are two troughs and an overflow pipe. From the spring the yellow-waymarked path

93

continues up towards a MASSIVE SCREE SLOPE and a very obvious peak beyond it, pointing up into the sky. The route zigzags up over a firm scree base, and there are cairns en route as well. Some 18 minutes past the spring, the path flattens out for a short distance. A large rock offers some shade.

Eventually you will reach the **Afhenas Col** (④; **1h55min**). Here it may well be very windy indeed, but the thrill of being up so high and seeing for miles and miles is terrific. On a clear day, looking back to Kallergi, you might just be able to pick out Theodorou Island to the left of the refuge, off the distant north coast. *(The Shorter walk turns back from here, and the E4 leaves us too, to head west and eventually south to Sougia.)*

The climb to the Gingilos summit starts from this ridge. Look left to find an arrow pointing up the edge of the mountain. In fact there are two waymarked routes up to the top; choose whichever looks easiest for you. (The route to the left passes closest to a dangerous pit: see 'Caution' below.) Either way, follow the yellow way-marking — do not lose sight of it — and it will lead you steeply upwards. In places it is necessary to clamber and scramble; you need to be very surefooted and confident. *Caution:* After about 100m/yds there is a sheer-sided

pit just to the right below the marked path — it's about 2.5m/ 8ft in diameter and it plummets 115m/375ft straight down! It is marked off with a few iron stakes, but *beware — especially on the descent!*

Before long you will have a simply splendid view over the Omalos again and, by **2h25min**, the route will become easier as you near the top. Soon you will almost be at the top of this magnificent mountain, by a LARGE CAIRN ON A FLAT AREA* (⑥).* Go left, *carefully,* to the marginally higher SUMMIT OF **Gingilos** (**2h30min**), marked by a METAL ROD (the remains of a cross) and a SHRINE.

When you have taken in the tremendous view, make your way back to the Afhenas Col by carefully following the way-marking from the large cairn on the flat. It offers a choice of routes, some easier than others. Use your discretion, knowing where you are heading. Fifty minutes later you will be back at the ridge. It's pleasant, on the way down, to be able to pay more attention to the spectacular landscape and the trees — among them the pretty Montpelier maple. It takes about 2h30min to descend back to **Xiloskala** (**5-6h**). Sit down by the café/shop in the CAR PARK (◉), so you are near where the bus turns round (rapidly) and leaves almost immediately.

---

*If you plan to continue to Volakias, walk downhill slightly from this CAIRN, heading south, and traverse to the next saddle, from where you have another ascent of 250m/820ft to the Volakias summit, 45 minutes from Gingilos. From the saddle

work your way *carefully* round the *left side* of the obvious ridge of outcropping rocks (there are some small CAIRN WAYMARKERS). (In mountaineering circles up here, Gingilos is considered 'superior' to the higher peak of Volakias, so don't feel the *need* to press on!)

Walk 20: A HIGH MOUNTAIN CIRCUIT FROM KALLERGI

Distance: 12km/7.4mi; 6h45min (19km/12mi from/ back to Xiloskala)

Grade: ● for experienced hill-walkers: strenuous, with overall ascents/descents of about 900m/ 2950ft. Almost no shade. Partly along the E4 trail

Equipment: walking boots, windproof, sunhat, scarf, GPS or compass, picnic, ample water

Picnic: near Kallergi or the Poria (meagre shade)

Access: 🚗 4WD vehicle (preferably) to/from Kallergi (35° 19.287′N, 23° 55.900′E), or stay overnight there (see under 'Short walk', page 97). Alternatively, 🚌 or 🚐 to/from Xiloskala (see Walk 19, page 92), then walk to and from Kallergi (add 370m/1215ft of ascent and 3h10min; see Short walk on page 98). This option should only be undertaken by very fit walkers.

Short walk: Xiloskala — Kallergi — Xiloskala (6.8km/ 4.2mi; 3h10min). ● Although mostly on a gravel track, it's quite a pull up (ascent of 370m/ 1210ft). Walking trainers, sunhat, picnic, water. Access/ return: as Walk 19, page 92. See

A breathtaking hike in more ways than one, the trek to Melindaou is, without doubt, worth the effort. The lure of the high mountains is a compelling experience, and this walk — in the heart of the splendid Levka Ori (White Mountains) — is an exciting introduction to high mountain walking on Crete. This expedition requires stamina. You must also be sure-footed and know how to use a compass or GPS competently. The rewards are ample, and walking in this area, we are sure, will mean the beginning of a long association with Crete's mountains. You will carry the views with you forever — the space, the fold upon fold of rock and mountainside, the colours and textures, the height, depth and strength of Western Crete.

Before setting off, be sure to tell someone at Kallergi where you are going. Then **start out**: walk the length of the southern, front side of the **Kallergi** REFUGE (◎) and follow the short path leading to a gravel track. This track heads off east towards the

The walker is a mere dot in the landscape on this high mountain walk which circles Mavri (the central peak). Melindaou is to the right.

mountains. You will follow it to the Poria ('Shepherds' Saddle') along the well-marked E4 route. The E4 cuts the first bend off the track by descending a stepped path on the right about 400m from Kallergi. When you rejoin the gravel track, be aware that it is also used by cross-country bikers travelling at speed. The route affords a tremendous view of Kallergi and Gingilos — as you can see in the photograph on page 98.

Some **25min** from Kallergi, when the hut is completely out of sight, and the valley falls away to the left of the track, you will have a wonderful view of mountains … and still more mountains. From here, on a clear day, it is possible to see all the way to Theodorou Island off the north coast, west of Hania. Then (**45min**), for a good view of Gingilos and Volakias, go right off the track (at a break in the fence).

In under **1h** from Kallergi, rounding a bend in the track, you will be at a SADDLE (**1**), called '**Poria**' by the shepherds. Leave the track here, and head right on the well-waymarked path (there is a building up to the right). After 50 minutes of climbing, much of which is steep, the route flattens out briefly; you will be level with the refuge, now far in the distance. This respite doesn't last long, however, and the route continues on and up, beyond a substantial CAIRN.

Fifteen minutes later, reach the top of the first ridge, from where you can feast your eyes upon yet more splendid mountains and the inspiring Cretan landscape. Head left along the ridge in a northeasterly direction and

follow the waymarking. As the route rises again, *follow the waymarking assiduously.* Ten minutes later you will be on the SUMMIT OF **Psari** (**2**; **2h**), marked by a short CONCRETE PILLAR with bits of iron protruding from it. From this point you can see the route leading across towards Mavri (the photograph on page 95 was taken here and shows the route clearly).

Setting off from the concrete pillar, continue north-northeast. In just under 10 minutes, start to climb again. Fifteen minutes later, CAIRNS mark the way, as the route skirts round to the right of **Mavri** (**3**), below the summit. At **2h40min**, having gone halfway along the next ridge, notice the path heading sharply back to the left, round the north side of Mavri (marked with an E4 POLE; **4**). This is the homeward route. You can either head back now or continue the main walk to Melindaou.

Ten minutes before the summit the walk flattens out — and then you're there! E4 poles lead you across the southern slope and you can leave the main E4 path and head diagonally up to the

SUMMIT OF **Melindaou** (**5**; **3h20min**).

While the E4 continues past Melindaou, there is no obvious point of return for day-walkers; the path leads on even further into the White Mountains, to Pahnes, the highest peak in the range — a couple of days' and nights' trek away. So unless you're with a guide, it's best to return to the homeward path, which you identified after passing Mavri.

From the E4 POLE (**4**) it cuts a route lower down and back across the north side of the mountain, in the direction of Kallergi. Follow the waymarking poles over a ridge and look down to the right, along the valley ahead: you will spot a clear path. Pick your way carefully down towards the path and the valley floor — a rough descent lasting 15 minutes. Take care to steer clear of any beehives if you're walking here in summer.

Once on the floor of the valley, more E4 waymarking will guide you back to your outgoing track, not far from the point where you started up the mountainside. In April and May the valley floor is swathed in crocuses and wild-flowers — a heartening sight for the trek back to Kallergi. Well into the return, the path crosses a dried-up watercourse and continues unevenly all the way back to the track. Turn left and

walk via the scattered shepherds' dwellings at the **Poria** (**1**) back to **Kallergi** (**O**; **6h45min**); the sense of achievement is terrific.

Short walk (to Kallergi) _____

Kallergi is the mountain refuge in the Levka Ori that hikers and climbers use as a base for exploring the range, under the guidance and supervision of the refuge's professional Austrian management. However, you don't have to be an expert to enjoy its spectacular position, perched like an eyrie at 1677m/ 5470ft above sea level. You can spend a night by booking ahead (tel: 28210 44647; www. eoshanion.gr) — or simply visit to marvel at the views, enjoy a picnic and revel in the peaceful atmosphere of the mountains.

The path to Kallergi is marked from the CAR PARK at **Xiloskala** (**1**) by an INFORMATION BOARD at the left of the entrance to the Samaria Gorge. Follow the red arrow, immediately going through a GATE. The path crosses the hillside diagonally, climbing very gradually at first and running almost parallel with the car park and road below. Look back across the car park and beyond the tourist pavilion, to Gingilos, the impressive grey mass in the background. As the path rounds the shoulder of the hill, the Omalos comes into view, spread out like a tablecloth far below.

The Kallergi refuge sits in a splendid position, looking out to Gingilos (Walk 19) and the White Mountains; below these heights, the Samaria Gorge slices its way to the sea. You're very likely to see 'kri kri' in this area — wild mountain goats. The refuge provides an authentic retreat from the noisy world we live in and offers simple, clean, comfortable accommodation and facilities, with an evening meal and breakfast. To book, see details under 'Short walk' on page 97.

return. Go through the stock control fence and follow the track uphill to the right. (Ten minutes up the track, at the first big left-hand bend, the adventurous might like to follow the blue waymarking up the ravine. This scramble requires care, is no faster than the track route, and is *not* recommended as a descent.)

Just before the track reaches the top, there is a shrine, an igloo-shaped stone SHEPHERDS' SHELTER and the beginning of E4 POLE WAYMARKING. The track divides at this shelter; take the right-hand fork and walk a further 150m/yds to the **Kallergi** refuge (○), reached in **1h45min**.

Return the same way.

Continue on the path until it meets a rough gravel track on a hairpin bend (Ⓑ; **40min**). A small cairn marks the junction; this waymarker is a help on the

Walk 21: THE SAMARIA GORGE

See also photographs opposite, pages 22-23, 111 and cover
Distance: 15km/9.3mi; 4-6h
Open: April/May to October (depending on rainfall); there is a charge to enter; pick up an English leaflet on payment.
Important note: Do not try to find an alternative route to the sea; stay on the designated path through the gorge. *This is imperative.* Swimming in the rock pools is forbidden; console yourself with the thought of a swim at the end of the walk.
Grade: ● straightforward but strenuous, particularly if you are not used to walking; the descent is 1250m/4100ft. You must be sure-footed crossing the bed on slippery stones. Plenty of shade in the upper gorge, but full sun for the last half hour.
Equipment: walking trainers or walking boots, sunhat, water bottle (for collecting spring water), picnic, swimming things
Picnic: throughout the gorge
Access: 🚌 to Omalos (Timetable 3); journey time about 45min (get off at the last stop, Xiloskala). Return by ⛴ to Hora Sfakion, departs Agia Roumeli 15.45, 16.30, 17.00, 17.45; voyage time 1h30min. Then 🚌 from Hora Sfakion (Timetable 4); journey time about 2h

The Samaria Gorge may be one of the reasons why you have come to Crete. Even if it isn't, you will soon hear tell of it; few people can resist the lure of Europe's longest gorge. And you won't be disappointed if you can see through the people! Setting out *very* early (the gorge opens at 6am) is the best way to avoid the crowds. Although this walk follows a well-trodden path, walking the gorge requires stamina, and *robust footwear is essential*.

Enough about caution. Here's some scene-setting: the landscape is simply spectacular, from the top of the gorge at Omalos to the bottom at Agia Roumeli — and all along the south coast on your boat trip to Hora Sfakion (where you'll find your bus back to Hania and the north coast). The White Mountains tower around you as the route leads seawards under shady pine trees through which sunlight slants. You'll pass cool pools and cross wide-open stretches of ancient, bleached rocky river bed.

Imagine light and shadow; height and depth; rock in shades of grey, green, blue and brown; mountains, trees and sky; birdsong and silence. It's a special experience walking through this natural wonder. If you walk the gorge in springtime, the wild flowers are another bonus to the excursion. At whatever time of year you walk the gorge, don't go down helter-skelter, trying to beat any records. Go at a leisurely pace and take in your surroundings. We haven't given any times for reaching specific points on the walk for this very reason. Enjoy the day.

The bus drops you in the **Samaria Gorge** CAR PARK (**○**), by shops and a *cafeneion* with a WC, where you can 'regroup' before starting out. Then buy your ticket; hang on to it. Half will be taken from you at the end of the gorge; it helps wardens to ascertain if everyone has gone through the gorge at the end of the day and, of course, it aids 'statistics'.

Start the walk on the **Xiloskala**, the wooden staircase down into the gorge — a solid construction made of tree trunks. Doubtless there will be a mass of other people setting off with you (up to 3000 people *a day* walk Samaria in high summer), which isn't encouraging, but the crowd thins out as people either turn back or establish their individual pace and walk and stop and walk again, marvelling at this splendid achievement of nature.

The first eye-catcher is Gingilos Mountain (see photograph on page 98) — a huge wall of rock towering majestically up to the right. You may well have already climbed Gingilos (Walk 19); it's a tremendous feeling to see the mountain from down here, particularly if you have been to the top …

The staircase becomes a path and drops very steeply about 600m (almost 2000ft) to the bottom of the upper gorge. There are ample SPRINGS, TABLES, and WCs en route (see map), so picnicking possibilities abound. Once you've passed the small chapel of **Agios Nikolaos** (**❶**), nestling amongst pines and cypresses to the right, the route becomes less steep. When you reach the **Samaria rest area** (**❷**) and the old hamlet of **Samaria**

(**❸**), you will be about halfway to the sea. One of the buildings (into which you can go and sign the VISITORS' BOOK) has been restored for the wardens who replaced the original inhabitants when the gorge was designated a national park.

From Samaria, continue on towards the sea, past the **Ossia Maria** church. The path twists and turns in places, allowing for rock formations and geological contortion, crossing the watercourse by stepping-stones in some places. You will know when you reach the famous **Sideroportes** (**❹**; 'Iron Gates', shown opposite) — where the gorge is at its narrowest. You're at about 150m/500ft here, with rock walls soaring hundreds of metres above you on either side. Beyond this point the scenery opens out.

There are TICKET COLLECTORS and refreshment KIOSKS (**❺**) a couple of kilometres before road comes underfoot at **Palea (Old) Agia Roumeli.** This village was abandoned due to flash flooding: the **Tarraios River** is so full in winter that the gorge has to be closed. Cross to the cemetery church of **Agia Triada**; a FERRY SHUTTLE BUS runs from here in high season. Eventually you come into **Agia Roumeli** itself (keep left at the first fork and right at the second) — perhaps somewhat weary and ready for a refreshing swim in the Libyan Sea, before taking the ferry (**○**) to Hora Sfakion. Weary or not, you will feel exhilarated beyond measure; 'walking Samaria' is an unforgettable achievement. You might even stay the night here and carry on to Loutro tomorrow (Walk 22).

Xilóskala

Neroutsiko rest area

E4

Riza Sikiás rest area

WC

Ágios Nikólaos

Vrísi rest area

Gíngilos
1974

E4

Samariá rest area

WC

Ágios Geórgios

Óssia María
Samariá

Néro tís Perdíkas rest area

Samaria Gorge

Aféndis Christós

Christós rest area

WC

Checkpoint

Agía Paraskeví
Pálaia Agía Rouméli

Agía Triáda

SOÚGIA

Agía Rouméli

Walk 22: FROM AGIA ROUMELI TO LOUTRO

Map continues on page 106

Distance: 15km/9.3mi; 5h05min

Grade: ●: moderate-strenuous, with some scrambling; ascents/ descents of 300m/1000ft overall; possibility of vertigo on one short stretch. E4-waymarked

Equipment: walking trainers, sunhat, picnic, water, swimming things

Picnic: Agios Pavlos

Access: 🚌 to Hora Sfakion (Timetable 4); journey time

about 2h. Then 🚢 to Agia Roumeli: departs Hora Sfakion daily at 10.30, 13.00, 16.50, 18.00; voyage time 1h30min. Return by 🚢 from Loutro to Hora Sfakion: departs daily at 09.30, 10.30, 11.30, 12.30, 13.30, 16.00, 17.00, 18.10; voyage time 30min. Then 🚌 to Hania (Timetable 4; buses connect with the boats); journey time about 2h

Alternative walks: Combine this with Walk 21, 23 or 24.

The gorgeous hike between Agia Roumeli and Hora Sfakion splits nicely into two, and that's how we describe it. But whether you undertake it as one walk or two, do start out early, to benefit from the early morning cool. The first stage of the walk has some shade, but the leg from Loutro to Hora Sfakion (Walk 24) is virtually devoid of it. High cliffs form a towering wall to the left, sometimes close at hand, edging the path, elsewhere set back in high

majesty. Moving east, you will skirt or cross beaches, walk under pine trees — scrunching their needles and inhaling the heady scent, edge along high, but safe cliff paths, and scramble over boulders. With the sparkling sea hemming your route on the right, you'll have lovely swimming opportunities.

Agia Roumeli is a very pleasant place to stay overnight, *after* the Samaria Gorge-walkers have left with the last boat. The same is true of Loutro and Lykkos (the ancient port of Fenix, just west of Loutro). All have rooms for rent.

Start out from the FERRY (○) by walking to the middle of **Agia Roumeli**, and then towards the bottom of the **Samaria Gorge**. Either wade

across the **Tarraios River** or cross it via the VENETIAN BRIDGE (❶), then continue on the WAY-MARKED E4 PATH. Beyond the inconspicuous mouth of the

102

Eligias Gorge, you come to a small TAVERNA and then the lovely Byzantine church of **Agios Pavlos** (❷; **1h25min**). About half an hour from this point, keep to the lower path (the upper one goes to Agios Ioannis; ❹).

In under four hours you will have a stiff pull up and scramble, before arriving at gorgeous **Marmara** (Marble) **Bay** at the mouth of the **Aradhena Gorge** (Walk 23) — perfect for a swim or a rest. Vertigo sufferers may find the going a bit testing on a short section of exposed path (**4h**) between Marmara and **Lykkos Bay**.

Then you are on the last leg: the route goes across the terrace of the last TAVERNA and up steps. Once over the next hill you will be able to see Livaniana (Walk 23) up to the left and, down to the right, what used to be the ancient port of **Fenix**, where there is now a pleasant taverna. Continue on the waymarked path straight ahead, above Fenix, to pass the VENETIAN CASTLE in its commanding position and then reach the haven of **Loutro** (❍; **5h05min**). Alternatively, round the headland from FENIX BEACH: this involves one more short climb past the castle (adds 10 minutes).

Take a break — or spend the night — at delightful Loutro.

See also photograph page 103
Distance: 18km/11.2mi;
7h05min

Grade: ●● straightforward but
strenuous, with 650m/2150ft of
ascents/descents, some quite
steep. You must be sure-footed
and have a head for heights
(possibility of vertigo). Various
waymarks, including E4
Equipment: walking trainers,
sunhat, picnic, water, swimming
things
Picnic: Aradhena Gorge (shade)
Access: 🚐 to Hora Sfakion
(Timetable 4); journey time
about 2h. Then ⛴ to Loutro:
departs Hora Sfakion daily at
10.00, 11.00, 12.00, 13.00,
14.00, 16.30, 17.30, 18.30;
voyage time 30min. Return by
⛴ from Loutro to Hora
Sfakion: departs daily at 09.30,
10.30, 11.30, 12.30, 13.30,
16.00, 17.00, 18.10; voyage
time 30min. Then 🚐 to Hania
(Timetable 4; buses connect
with the boats); journey time
about 2h

**Optional start: Loutro head-
land.** ●● This optional way to
start any of the walks adds 10
minutes. At the western end of
Loutro go up steps at the left of
the Hotel Daskalogiannis (**❶**),
signposted 'PATH TO VENETIAN
CASTLE, ROMAN REMAINS').
Walk over the terrace of the
Porto Loutro Hotel 2 and go
through a gate, then continue
past the Roman remains and the
CHURCH AND CEMETERY to the
left on the headland. Some
15min from Loutro, where a
sewage CISTERN interrupts the
path, continue by following the
blue dots. Before long you will
see Livaniana tucked up into the
hillside ahead, to the right.
When you arrive at **Fenix Beach**

(30min), head for the CHURCH
WITH ITS TWO PALM TREES. Go
through a gate and curl up
behind the church in a gentle
bend, and continue west and
uphill until you meet the well-
waymarked E4 route.

**Shorter walk: Loutro —
Aradhena Gorge — Livaniana
— Loutro** (10km/6.2mi;
4h05min). ●● Grade, equipment,
access/return as main walk (but
only half the climbing). Follow
the main walk to the junction at
2h45min, on the outskirts of
Livaniana (**❹**). Instead of
turning sharply left here, follow
the waymarking down through
the houses. There is a taverna
with a tremendous view on the
far side of the village — the only
sign of life! Just past the taverna
the track to Lykkos descends to
the right. Do *not* take this, but
continue for another 50m/yds,
climbing a little, until you
come to the old donkey trail
(**ⓑ**) on your right, waymarked
in blue. Follow this as it zigzags
down to the **Fenix** tavernas,
then head for the CHURCH WITH
TWO PALM TREES. Go through a
gate, curl up behind the church
in a gentle bend and continue
uphill until you meet the E4.
Now retrace your outgoing
route back to **Loutro** (**❍**).

Alternative walks
1 Combined Walks 21-24
(requires overnight stays at Agia
Roumeli and Loutro or Fenix).
First descend the Samaria
Gorge; walk on to Loutro the
next day, do this walk, then carry
on to Hora Sfakion.
**2 Loutro — Livaniana —
Aradhena Gorge — Loutro**
(11km/6.8mi; 4h15min). ●●
Grade, equipment, access/return
as main walk (but ascent/descent

of 350m/1150ft). This is a good choice if you want to relax at beautiful Marmara Beach at the end of the day, but the steep descent from Livaniana and down the gorge is quite taxing. Start out by walking to **Fenix Beach** via the headland at Loutro (❶; see 'Optional start' above). Beyond Fenix, when you meet the waymarked E4 route (❻), cross over and continue steeply uphill to the right. The way peters out into a path and then becomes an old blue-waymarked donkey trail zigzagging neatly uphill. There is a great view as you ascend. When you reach the outskirts of **Livaniana**, walk up onto a ROAD. You can rest or replenish your water supply in the small taverna on the left. Then take the waymarked zigzag path and steps up through the village. The path passes an old outdoor oven and meets the chicken wire above the village CHURCH (❹; 1h30min). Continue above the church, making for the gorge (faded blue waymarking). Head

down towards terraced olive trees and, after passing between wooden gateposts, turn left. Descend steeply through more olive tree terracing until you reach the dry stream bed (❷; by a large solitary olive tree). Here the path crosses to the other side of the gorge. Make your way down through the boulder-strewn gorge (cairns and various waymarking colours) to **Marmara Beach** (3h). Then take the E4 path east to **Loutro** (❻; 4h15min).

3 Loutro — Livaniana — Aradhena — Anopolis — Loutro (13km/8mi; 5h50min).
●❗ Grade, equipment, access/return as main walk. If you want to enjoy Marmara Beach another day (when you can either walk a short way up the Aradhena Gorge or follow the Shorter walk above), then omit the gorge. Follow ALTERNATIVE WALK 2 to the church in **Livaniana** (❹; 1h30min). Then pick up the main walk at the 2h45min-point and follow it to the end, saving 1h15min.

This is a glorious combination of coast, seaside village, gorge and mountain village, which can be done in many different ways. We prefer to walk two-thirds of the way *up* the lower gorge (enjoying the best part of it), and then come back *downhill* to Loutro via Anopolis — since this last section is long, steep and exposed. But if you stay overnight in Loutro you will no doubt meet people who walk *up* to Anopolis, on to Aradhena, and *down the whole gorge* or vice versa. They follow a high zig-zagging path cut into the side of the upper gorge. Although this path bypasses the original steel ladders bolted to the rock face, it could still be challenging for vertigo-sufferers. Our map shows the route in detail, although we don't describe it.

Start the walk from the middle of the beach (❻) in **Loutro**. Walk into the village, passing to the right of the KIOSK on the

beach. Turn left by Sofia's mini-market, then head round to the left (blue waymarking) on the obvious path running in an arc behind the village. Pass houses on your right and walk through a gate, just after which you will see an E4 SIGN on an ancient olive tree. Ignore a turning to the left (by a SHRINE on the left). Continue winding up the path, ignoring gates to the left; follow the blue waymarking. At a junction, where the VENETIAN CASTLE RUINS are signposted to the left, keep right for 'FENIX' on the E4 path. The path follows the wall surrounding the castle ruins and leads to the brow of the hillside. The village tucked up into the hillside ahead, to the right, is Livaniana, which you will skirt later in the walk. Soon your complete coastal route can be seen stretching out in front of you.

As you start descending, **Fenix Beach** comes into view — a smattering of blue and white tavernas and rooms for rent. The route zigzags down behind them, leaving a whitewashed CHURCH WITH TWO PALM TREES down to the left. Just past the church, cross diagonally over a track. (Some 350m/yds past here, at a Y-fork (**C**), Alternative walks 2 and 3 climb to Livaniana on a blue-waymarked donkey trail, and the Shorter walk descends this trail.) Continue on the well-waymarked E4 path in the general direction of the coast. Before long you are over the next small headland (where there are more tavernas with rooms to rent) and down by the sea at **Lykkos Beach** (**30min**).

Keep straight on downhill, hugging the rocks on your left. Descend amidst the line of buildings. The path heads down some concrete steps, across taverna terraces, and then across a flat pebbly stretch behind a beach. The last building en route is a restaurant. Walk along this beach to the next cove, at the far side of which there is an E4 SIGN. Here steps hewn out of the rock take you steeply up onto the cliffs (you'll have to use your hands in places). You need to *go*

carefully here, as the path curls tightly up to the right, past a cave. Where the path is difficult to discern, YELLOW PAINT DAUBS identify the route. Those who suffer from vertigo will find this exposed stretch the most difficult part of the walk.

Once over the next headland you will be looking down over **Marmara** (Marble) **Beach**, beyond which are a few buildings and a small CHURCH. The path descends to a flatter area and bears left to this beach (**1h15min**) with its crystal-clear, inviting water.

From here *ignore* the E4 signs, which now lead along the coast (the route of Walk 22). Instead, head inland, following a stream bed into the mouth of the **Aradhena Gorge**. The atmosphere changes rapidly as huge rock faces tower either side of the route, providing cooling shade. Five minutes into the gorge, the magnificent rock wall on your right has a cave at its base. Follow the twists and turns of the stream bed. By **1h25min** it looks as if a massive boulder blocks the way (**❶**) — perhaps it's the 'plug' that has come out of the mountainside above and ahead, leaving a cave? Follow waymarking (faded red and blue, newer green/red) to the right of the boulder, scrambling over a huge rockfall for five minutes. Then, to get back down to the stream bed, head towards the

left-hand rock wall. CAIRNS will show you the way back to the stream bed, where you pick up the red waymarking again. Continue through a thicket of bushes. Waymarking will direct you around another rockfall, as you climb more steeply.

At **1h50min** a WATER TROUGH and a large oleander bush make a peaceful resting spot in amongst the rocks. Beyond here, look for waymarking on the left-hand side of the gorge, pointing uphill, away from the trough, and taking you into another scramble. Follow the way-marking carefully! Five minutes from the water trough the path flattens out, and the landscape opens up. A well-painted boulder (mostly red/green stripes) comes into sight on the left. Follow the arrow indicating 'LIVANIANA' — to the right. You skirt round a LARGE OLIVE TREE (**❷**; **2h**), as you climb up the right-hand side of the gorge. You will spot some faded blue waymarking as the path winds up the hillside through old terraced olive trees towards the rock face on your right.

Having hugged the rock face, the steep path rises to a LARGE WALLED ENCLOSURE WITH CHICKEN WIRE ON TOP (**❸**) directly in front of you. Turn left, keeping it close by on your right, and continue uphill through more terracing. Then turn right through a gap in the drystone wall. Continue to follow the waymarking. A few minutes after the gap in the wall, the path turns left, following a stone wall. A minute later there is a wonderful view down over the coast, and the CHURCH (❹) at **Livaniana** is just a few metres ahead of you. This is the upper part of the almost-deserted village of Livaniana, and you are at a junction (**2h45min**). *(The Shorter walk goes straight ahead here.)*

The main walk turns *sharply left*, avoiding the village: walk between the wall with chicken wire on the left and the wire fence on the right — you may notice a red waymark. The rocky path climbs along the right-hand side of a wall; keep beside the wall. When the walled and fenced enclosure ends, the waymarked path continues straight ahead. At this point you reach a rocky outcrop and, continuing along the ridge, you

Ruins at Aradhena, with a view to the White Mountains

encounter another stone wall: keep this wall on your right and head across an open area; the sea is now in sight again. Ahead you can see the stone walls supporting your ongoing path as it climbs the hillside.

At **3h05min** the path opens out on a flatter area; look carefully for the waymarking here — and later, as you start to climb again in zigzags. Watch for the griffon vultures that are often seen here — it will help take your mind off the long haul — and they are likely to be breathtakingly close. A road is visible ahead cutting across the hillside; the path joins the ROAD (**5**) at just under the **3h30min**-mark, after a fairly steep climb. Turn left on this dirt road and follow it in a bend to the right. There are magnificent views over Livaniana and the beaches below — you can see Lykkos, Fenix and part of Loutro.

Follow the road over the hill and onto a plateau. Under 20 minutes from where the path met this road you round a bend and have a wonderful view of the White Mountains ... marred only by a concrete animal shed in the foreground. Pass this shed, ignoring a fork off to the right just before it. Ten minutes later the road has turned away from the coast, behind the shed, and you are heading straight towards the mountains. Rock-strewn grazing land and animal enclosures lie off to the left.

The houses and old church of **Aradhena** come into sight (**4h15min**). When you arrive at a T-junction, turn left: you will see the IRON BRIDGE (**6**) that leads over the top of the gorge

into Aradhena (the photographs overleaf were taken from this point). It is also highly likely that you will see griffon vultures here. Crossing the bridge is not for vertigo sufferers; although robust and safe enough for vehicles, it is made with quite large gaps between the slats, and if a car goes past the whole thing vibrates loudly! The village, although mostly deserted, has signs of renovation. Until 1986 Aradhena was only approachable by the steep donkey paths visible down the sides of the gorge below. There is a small snack bar directly over the bridge, and the surroundings of the 14th-century church make a pleasant shaded place to sit. Or stay by the bridge to watch the bungee-jumpers...

To continue the walk, retrace your steps past the T-junction and keep straight ahead on the road. After three minutes, just before a stone wall, head right on a track, passing under power cables. After about 50 paces look carefully on the left for a cairn, placed almost directly below the power cables, just before a wall on which there are red waymarks. Follow the wall, and fork left under an ancient olive tree. You are now on a rough old cobbled path (**7**). Fifteen minutes from the T-junction the houses of Anopolis (still spelled with an 's' at the end, but pronounced Anopoli) come into view. At about this point the cobbles run out abruptly, but the waymarked path is clear as it heads downhill. Follow it between stone walls and turn left. Then, almost immediately (where the path meets a fence), walk left towards the houses of more of a circle, with a statue of Daskalogiannis in the middle. Head right and follow a sign for 'AG EIKATERINI'. Passing the last houses, the road goes on into a hairpin bend. There's a nice view looking back over the fertile plain around Anopolis.

Some 25 minutes from the square, when the road ends at a flat area, walk right towards a shrine. The path straight ahead here goes down to Loutro, 1h15min away. First, however, for an even more fantastic view and a very worthwhile detour, climb steeply up to the right from the shrine, to the church of **Agia Eikaterina** (❽) with a fine viewing platform. Then return to the path and descend *carefully* to Loutro; this path requires steady footwork. Ten minutes from the shrine ignore a path forking left, back to Anopolis. Some minutes later, join a bulldozed track. Head down to the right and after about 100m/yds cairns on the left signal where you rejoin the path. When you next meet the track, more cairns point the way (straight over). The path crosses a gully.

Some 25 minutes later you come to a fork: the right fork goes to 'Finix'. Take the *left* fork, down to Loutro. Fifteen minutes later pass a SHRINE (❻) on the left (where Walk 24 begins) and head right, towards the village. Clamber through a stock control gate and in five minutes (**7h05min**) you're back in **Loutro** (◯) — more than ready for a swim, as you have probably been out for more like 10 hours!

Anopolis. You come onto a road; follow this as it makes a tight bend to the right. Pass a small chapel on the left, surrounded by lovely shady holm oaks and, when you come to a T-junction, turn right on another road.

After 15 minutes, at a T-junction (where there is a taverna on the left), turn right to the village 'square' in **Anopolis** (**5h**). It is

Walk 24: FROM LOUTRO TO HORA SFAKION

See map pages 106-107; see
also photograph page 103
Distance: 7km/4.3mi; 2h
Grade: ●: moderate, with some
scrambling (although there are
no appreciable climbs/descents);
you must be sure-footed and
have a head for heights
(possibility of vertigo). E4-
waymarked. *Very little shade*
Equipment: walking trainers,
sunhat, picnic, water, swimming
things

Picnic: Sweetwater beach
(springs and some shade)
Access: 🚌 to Hora Sfakion
(Timetable 4); journey time
about 2h. Then ⛴ to Loutro:
see Walk 23, page 104; voyage
time 30min. Return by 🚌 from
Hora Sfakion (Timetable 4; as
above)
Alternative walk: Tack this on
to Walk 22 (7h05min) — or
stay overnight in the area to
explore Walks 21 and 23 as well.

Loutro is a wonderful, away-from-it-all backwater, perfect for really relaxing — particularly as there is no
traffic, bar boats. From the ferry you will see the route
heading east along the hillside above the coast.

Start the walk at **Loutro**
HARBOUR (○): head up to the
left of the Taverna Kri-kri, at the
east end of the bay. The coastal
path starts at an easily-visible
SHRINE (◎). (Walk 23 comes
directly down the hillside in
zigzags to this point.) Those
who suffer from vertigo may
experience difficulty in **15min**,
as the path skirts the edge of the
steep cliff, and again at the
30min-point, where you cross a
stretch of sandy scree.
Pass **Agios Stavros** chapel and
descend to **Sweetwater Beach**
(**1h**). Fresh springs gush from

the mountainside here, and
there are boats to and from
Loutro and Hora Sfakion in
high season. Continue over
beach and rocks; **1h20min** from
Loutro the path runs some
70m/200ft or more above the
sea, and there is a sheer drop
down to the right. This
potentially vertiginous stretch
lasts for 10-12 minutes.
When the path meets road, on a
hairpin bend, turn right and
walk into **Hora Sfakion** (○;
2h). You reach the BUS STOP —
and a host of other amenities —
just as you come into the village.

*Hora Sfakion from the sea. There are regular sailings to Loutro, Agia
Roumeli, Sougia and Paleohora.*

Walk 25: THE IMBROS GORGE • KOMITADES • HORA SFAKION

See also photographs pages 29, 111

Distance: 12km/7.4mi; 3h50min

Note: there is a small fee payable to enter the gorge.

Grade: ● fairly straightforward descent of 750m/2460ft in a gorge, but you must be sure-footed and agile

Equipment: walking trainers or boots, sunhat, picnic, water, swimming things

Picnic: in the shady gorge

Access: Hora Sfakion 🚌 to Imbros (Timetable 4); journey time about 1h45min. *Hint:* Sit on the left-hand side of the bus for the best views. Or 🚗 to Imbros (parking near the entrance to the gorge). Return by 🚌 from Hora Sfakion to Hania (Timetable 4); journey time 1h45min. 🚗 Motorists will find an 8-seater minibus by the taverna at the end of the gorge, to take you back to your car at Imbros.

Shorter walk: Imbros Gorge — Komitades (7km/4.3mi; 2h50min). ● Grade, equipment, access as main walk. Follow the main walk to Komitades and catch a Frangokastello–Hora Sfakion 🚌 there: buses depart about 14.15 and 16.50; *recheck at Hora Sfakion!* journey time 10min. Then 🚌 as above.

This is a really delightful amble through the now popular, pine tree-lined Imbros Gorge, which narrows and widens very dramatically in places — until you reach the south coast and the Libyan Sea. The bus rides are quite long, since you follow a winding route from the north to south coast and then back again, but these journeys enable you to see a good slice of Cretan countryside. It's a good walk for children, too.

Make it clear that you'll be walking the **Imbros Gorge**, and the bus will drop you at the start, by a TAVERNA in **Imbros** village (○). (There is another bus stop and parking area further south by another taverna; (❷): see map.) **Start out** by taking the lane beside the 'IMBROS GORGE' sign, and after 250m turn right on a track. This track becomes a footpath as it meets the stream bed.

At first the surroundings are not very gorge-like; soon after collecting your ticket you will be surrounded by Jerusalem sage, striking in spring and early summer (see opposite). The route leads all the way to the coast; sometimes the path is in

the gorge, sometimes it runs beside it to avoid large boulders. Once you are on the route, it's virtually impossible to lose your way. Anywhere around here is a good place to picnic. By **50min** into the walk, you will be briefly on a donkey trail, the old main donkey trail to Sfakia, still beautifully cobbled.

Just past the NARROWEST PART OF THE GORGE (❶; where you can touch the walks on both sides), there's a small REST AREA; in summer, you may find enterprising people here selling raki and ouzo, well as cooling drinks.

At **2h20min** you can see the south coast and the sea ahead in the middle distance. You should

112

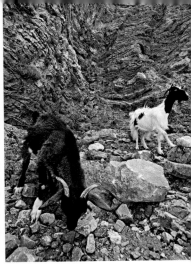

Jerusalem sage and wild goats in the Imbros Gorge

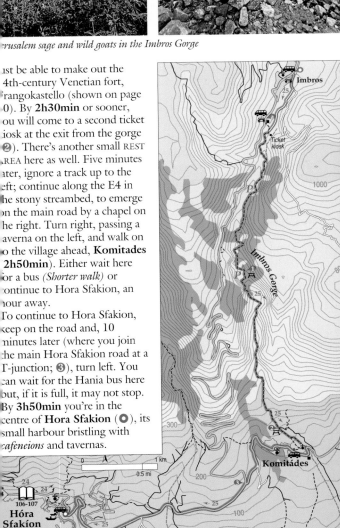

... ust be able to make out the 14th-century Venetian fort, Frangokastello (shown on page 0). By **2h30min** or sooner, you will come to a second ticket kiosk at the exit from the gorge ❷). There's another small REST AREA here as well. Five minutes later, ignore a track up to the left; continue along the E4 in the stony streambed, to emerge on the main road by a chapel on the right. Turn right, passing a taverna on the left, and walk on to the village ahead, **Komitades** (**2h50min**). Either wait here for a bus *(Shorter walk)* or continue to Hora Sfakion, an hour away.

To continue to Hora Sfakion, keep on the road and, 10 minutes later (where you join the main Hora Sfakion road at a T-junction; ❸), turn left. You can wait for the Hania bus here but, if it is full, it may not stop. By **3h50min** you're in the centre of **Hora Sfakion** (◯), its small harbour bristling with *cafeneions* and tavernas.

Walk 26: KARES (ASKYFOU) • ASFENDOS • AGIOS NEKTARIOS

Distance: 14.2km/8.8mi; 5h10min

Grade: ● moderate but long, with an ascent of about 300m/1000ft and descent of 950m/3100ft, the latter part in a gorge

Equipment: walking trainers, sunhat, picnic, water

Picnic: in a shady spot on the plain or round Goni

Access: Hora Sfakion 🚐 to 'Sfakian Bakery' junction in Askyfou (Timetable 4); journey time about 1h20min. (See main text for more detail about this bus stop.) Return by 🚐 from Agios Nektarios to Hora Sfakion (not in the timetables, but departs between 15.30-16.00 daily); journey time 20 minutes. Alternatively, pre-arrange a Sfakia taxi or call a taxi when you are nearing Ag Nektarios (tel: 28250 91269). Then 🚐 to Hania (Timetable 4); journey time about 2h

O ne of our favourite walks, this excursion combines a good bus ride, covering masses of ground, with a walk across the lovely plain shown on page 116 and then over some easy mountain terrain. We finish with a descent through a gorge, with the Libyan Sea as our goal. The road that the bus follows is the route along which thousands of war-weary soldiers trudged in 1941, when they withdrew, under relentless air attack, to the south coast. The walk leads you through a gorgeous chunk of Cretan countryside — spectacular anytime, but particularly picturesque in spring, when the plain at Askyfou is dotted with poppies and the gorge is lined with bright yellow Jerusalem sage.

Be ready to get off the bus when, having wound up and round hillsides, you see the Askyfou plain come into sight below left. Before you leave the bus, it passes an eye-catching old Turkish fort, strategically sited on a hillock mid-plain. Then the bus passes a first turn-off left to Kares; you want the *next* turn-off left for 'KARES', opposite the isolated 'Sfakian Bakery' on the main road (and just before the large domed church).

Start the walk from the BAKERY JUNCTION (**0**) in **Askyfou**: head south down into the hamlet of **Kares**, walking towards the plain and *forking right immediately,* following signs for the War Museum. Pass

114

the MUSEUM (**1**) on your right and head out of the village. Take the next left turning, a surfaced track. This track will take you across the plain itself via fields of vegetables planted and tended by the Askyfou villagers. Within a few minutes, ignore a turn to the left, then pass a WELL on the left. Soon, at a cross-tracks, turn left, passing another old WELL. Some 15 minutes from Kares (**20min**) the track becomes asphalted as it meets a road. Join the road, keeping straight ahead. The road rises as you approach **Goni**, the next village, and then curves round to the right, skirting the village. It ends by an old building with 'No. 20' painted on it (**2**). There is a

The White Mountains (Levka Ori) from the Askyfou plain

WALK INFORMATION BOARD here, and GREEN/WHITE WAYMARKING begins. Take the earthen track straight ahead, to the right of the building. It bends round and away from Goni. Follow the track straight on, ignoring grassy tracks off. Some 30 minutes from Kares, Goni will be directly behind you, as you head south into the valley.

Ten minutes beyond Goni, keep right at a fork. Pass through any mesh gates; the route starts to rise. At **1h10min**, just past a SHEPHERD'S DWELLING (**3**) on the left, where the track divides, turn left and curl back on yourself. As you walk up this track, look for a path running below you on the left. You will need to find a way down onto this wide path, then follow it heading due south towards the 'V' ahead.

At **1h30min** look for a smaller path going off left at a CAIRN and a RED ARROW (**4**). The waymarked path climbs to an open grassy area, then levels out. Seven minutes later the path divides; go left (**5**; RED ARROW). Ahead on the hillside notice some stone walls that underpin the ongoing path. Aiming for those walls, follow the path past a WATER TROUGH and under two large kermes oaks. The way leads up and continues to the left on the stone-built section ahead. The footpath widens out on the walls, which zigzag up to the PASS (⑥; **1h45min**).

From here a well-established path gradually starts the descent to the sea. The route descends across another open grassy area, past an ANIMAL SHELTER and a group of trees set off to the left. Reaching the far side of the flat grazing land, you will catch sight of the distant sea for the first time. A stony track leads off from here, 30m/yds from the grassy area. Take the path which goes off to the right of the track. It descends, meeting the track again after 10 minutes. Cross the track and look for the rather indistinct path again. (It's worth taking the path as it is more direct and cuts some loops off the track.) At **2h40min** pass a WATER DEPOSIT on the left, and stay on the track. Be aware that you are heading for the V of the gorge ahead. When you meet an asphalt road on a bend, walk straight ahead; the very basic houses of **Asfendos** come into sight (**2h50min**). The village CHURCH is high up on the right. A few minutes later you come to a wire mesh animal gate; go through and turn left on the road to Kallikratis. Go straight over the next crossroads (⑦; signposted left to Rethimnon and Kallikratis, right to Hania and Hora Sfakion).

In three minutes the asphalt stops; continue on a path, past some old houses and on into the countryside again. The V becomes a U in the distance, the left-hand side of it opening outwards as you near the gorge. The path is thickly edged with Jerusalem sage — a glorious bright yellow mass in spring. About half an hour from Asfendos there are clear signs that part of this very old path was formerly paved. You can see the gorge now, ahead of you. Forty minutes from Asfendos (**3h20min**), you will see the sea in the cleft ahead, and scree comes in on the right. Five minutes further on, pass a way-marked boulder. The path then does a double bend and zigzags down the hillside. Although you are high, the gorge is too layered to pose any problems for vertigo sufferers.

Keep on zigzagging down the hillside amongst any goats and sheep that might be about. About 1h30min from Asfendos (**4h10min**) you will be able to see the beach and sea below and ahead of you. If you come to any forks in the path, just continue in the same direction, down the side of the gorge. Before long, you will find that the route criss-crosses the dry river bed. Ten minutes from the start of these river bed crossings, you will be high above the dry river bed again.

Some 2h20min from Asfendos (**5h**) the path divides; go left. After a few minutes a fence comes in from the right. The path comes down to a gravelly area, where there is a CONCRETE BUILDING on the left. Walk past the building and then between the few houses of **Agios Nektarios**, to the south coast road. A CHURCH lies to the left (**5h10min**). Turn right on the main road to head for Hora Sfakion, or meet a pre-arranged taxi here. A bus for Hora Sfakion will pass at about 16.00.

Walk 27: CIRCUIT VIA MONI PREVELI

Distance: 11.3km/7mi; 3h30min

Grade: ● easy-moderate, with descents/ascents of about 425m/1400ft; you must be sure-footed and agile on the path above the river and for the descent to Palm Beach.

Equipment: walking trainers, sunhat, picnic, water, swimming things, suitable dress for Moni Preveli (trousers for men, longish skirts for women)

Picnic: by the bridge at the start

Access: 🚗 to/from the arched bridge 3.5km southeast of Asomatos on the road to Moni Preveli (Car tour 6; 35° 10.441'N, 24° 27.958'E); there is plenty of parking — either by the roadside or over the new concrete bridge, by the side of the duck pond.

Alternative walks

1 to Palm Beach and return (10km/6mi; 2h30min). ● Grade as main walk (descent/ascent of about 300m/1000ft); equipment and access as main walk. Follow the main walk to the CAR PARK (❸). Leave the car park via the gate in the eastern fence (the pay booth is at the western side). Follow the path on the western

side of the river, with the river on your right and the asphalt road to the monastery on your left and above you. This path (later a track) goes back to the bridge where the walk began.

2 Circuit from Asomatos, for those travelling by bus (18km/11.2mi; 5h15min). ● Grade as main walk, but considerably longer and with descents/ascents of about 600m/2000ft overall; equipment as main walk. Access: Plakias 🚌 from Rethimnon to/from Asomatos (Timetable 15); the return bus leaves Asomatos a few minutes after departure from Plakias; journey time 35min. The bus drops you off in the centre of Asomatos by the junction to Plakias and Moni Preveli; follow the signposted road, turning left after 1.5km (ⓐ). After another 2km you come to the bridge where the main walk starts; pick up the notes below and return the same way. *NB: In summer only, you can catch a bus from Moni Preveli back to Rethimnon (Timetable 14); journey time 45min — thus halving the distance and saving the long ascent.*

This is a beautiful circuit, although rather long if you travel by bus. If you don't mind hitch-hiking or taking an extra bus, it can be cut short at various points should the heat prove too exhausting or the temptations of flopping on the beach too much.

Moni Preveli

📖
126

The walk starts at the stEEPLY ARCHED BRIDGE (◯) near the Taverna Gefyra (Gefyra means 'bridge' in Greek), on the road to Moni Preveli and Palm Beach. Walk in front of the taverna, following the gravel track (initially asphalted) along the east side of the **Megalopotamos** — one of the few rivers in Crete that flows all year round — a lovely picnic setting. You cross another, COBBLED BRIDGE in 10 minutes, and continue on the right-hand track. About five minutes or so later, pass a gated and locked turning right to a DERELICT MONASTERY (❶). A few metres/yards further on, turn right and right again

(beside a fence), dipping down into a gully. Follow the narrow path round the left side of the gully and cross a small watercourse. The path then continues on the other side of the gully, somewhat precipitous in places.

The path circles clockwise round this valley, well defined, with CAIRNS and occasional RED WAY-MARKS. As you make for the saddle ahead, you go through a stock control gate and then the path opens out to give you views back towards Asomatos. But a tall wire fence prevents you from getting close to the edge and looking down into the gorge. This fence continues, just to the

119

right of your path. Soon you pass under some electricity cables (**50min**). Just afterwards, near a small TRANSMITTER to your right, the Libyan Sea and Palm Beach at Preveli come into full view, looking *unbelievably* inviting.

Still with the fence on your right, follow the well-trodden path as it turns left. Where the fence bends sharply left and appears to block your path, walk to the left for a few metres/yards, to where the fence runs out, and just walk round the end of it. From here turn right (RED DOT WAYMARKS). Keep the fence on your right and take the well-worn path that appears to just

Palm (Preveli) Beach, the palm-fringed oasis where the Megalopotamos empties into the crystal-clear waters of the Libyan Sea.

drop over the edge of the steep terrain. Zigzag down this path, which demands agility and sure-footedness. As you descend you will see a large taverna (with road access) on the neighbouring beach. Keep descending, taking whichever route seems easiest, all the while keeping the fence to your right. You are heading for a PATH THAT LINKS THE TWO BEACHES (**2**).

When you reach it, turn right and five minutes later you arrive at **Palm Beach** (**1h15min**). After a swim and a rest, wade across the river to the far side of the beach (where there's a café/bar in summer) and climb the rocks at the water's edge here, rounding the headland. Then take the steps up to the top of the cliff.

Within about 20 minutes you emerge at a PARKING AREA (**3**). Leave it via the vehicle entrance. After about three minutes a BLUE SIGN on your left directs you through a gate towards Moni Preveli. You pass a building on your right, and from here a track between fences funnels you in the right direction. Go straight over a junction (another BLUE SIGN) and head up a slope towards the main road. Where you join the road take a few minutes to hop over the fence and look at the SHRINE TO PEACE AND REMEMBRANCE (**4**). Turn left on the road and in a couple of minutes you round a bend and the monastery is now in view, 10 minutes away. You can fill up with water at **Moni Preveli** (**2h**) and have a wander round, if you have the proper clothing with you. In *summer only,* you can catch a bus back to

Rethimnon here; it travels via Asomatos.

To continue, leave the monastery and walk back along the asphalt road to the first right-hand bend, here take the dirt road off to the left (or take the short cut shown on the map at (**5**). This dirt road winds its way up the hill to a saddle (**2h20min**) and down the other side. In another quarter of an hour you are just outside **Yianniou**. Take a sharp right on another track that goes downhill about 70m/yds before a FOUNTAIN/WATERING HOLE on your left (just before entering the village). Almost immediately you come to a T-junction by a white-washed church: turn right. Soon the track bends left and rises steeply.

At the crest of this hill, the track splits three ways. Turn left and pass the church of **Agia Paraskevi**, on a ridge. Some 150m past this church keep right downhill (**6**). Five minutes later, turn right and follow a gently-rippling irrigation channel down to the asphalt road at the derelict monastery of **Kato Preveli** (**7**; 'lower Preveli'). This original 'Moni Preveli' was abandoned at the time of the Ottoman conquest.

Turn left and continue on the asphalt road for 10 minutes, until you reach the STEEPLY ARCHED BRIDGE you crossed at the start of your walk (**○**; **3h30min**). Pick up your transport here or, if you came by bus, stay on the asphalt road for an hour, to return to Asomatos (remember to turn right at the next T-junction; **❸**).

Walk 28: ANO MEROS • TRIPITI • ANO MEROS

Distance: 9km/5.6mi; 4h
Grade: ●: fairly strenuous ascent and descent of 600m/1970ft. The final ascent is not waymarked and involves some clambering; you must be sure-footed and have a head for heights. *Little shade en route*
Equipment: walking trainers, long socks/trousers in spring, sunhat, windproof, picnic, water
Picnic: Kaloidena chapel
Access: 🚗 to/from Ano Meros: park in the main street, near the church (35° 11.237'N, 24° 39.659'E). If friends can take you to/collect

you from Ano Meros, you might use a 🚐 one way (not in the timetables: *Mon-Fri only;* journey 1h30min): departs Rethimnon 05.30, 14.30; departs Ano Meros 16.00.
Short walk: Kaloidena chapel (2.4km/1.5mi; 40min). ● Easy, with an ascent/descent of only 160m/500ft. A pleasant leg-stretcher during a car tour, this gives you a bit of exercise and leads to a pretty picnic spot with a spring and fine views. Follow the main walk for the first 20 minutes; return the same way.

K edros is the elongated mountain on the western side of the Amari Valley, rising to 1775m/5822ft. This walk takes you up its flanks to a viewpoint on a lesser peak, Tripiti, from where you will enjoy a tremendous outlook. (If you are driving, watch for 12th-century frescoed Moni Agios Ioannis Theologos — on the left between Gerakari and Ano Meros. Gerakari, by the way, was levelled by the Germans during World War II in retaliation for the abduction of General Kreipe — a story detailed in the books by Moss and Leigh Fermor recommended on page 6.)

Start out by leaving the CHURCH (○) of **Ano Meros** on your right: head south on the main road, towards Hordaki. Immediately you enjoy a fantastic outlook towards Psiloritis. Ignore the first small, stepped turning (by the telephone box) off to the right. Take the *next* right turn — well-paved steps signposted 'PATH TO KALOIDENA, TRIPITI'. At the top of the flight of steps turn left; then, almost immediately, go right. The concrete track rises steeply; when it ends, ignore the turning to the right and take the path on the left, heading uphill. Keep a wire fence close by on the right, and turn left when you come to a crossing wire fence. Walk over some small boulders and around

the end of another wire fence, to come to a gravel track opposite a large WATER TANK (❶; 8min).
Turn right on the track. Two minutes later stay on the main track, leaving another track off to the left. Head towards the mountains; there is a valley down to the right. In places you will see vestiges of old water-channelling down the middle of the track.
At **20min** fork off right to see the restored chapel of **Kaloidena** (❷) — part of a monastery destroyed by the Turks in 1821. The chapel, with its splendid view, is above a gated shady concrete picnic area, where a clear spring gushes by the gate. Looking out over the Amari

122

Valley you can still see part of the Platys River.

To continue the walk, head back to the fork in the track and head up to the right. At the next T-junction go left on an asphalt road, leaving an old farm building up to your right. There are the remains of an old WATERMILL down to the left just past the junction. After 200m you go through a GATEWAY and pass a track off to the left; turn sharp right immediately, on a weak track (there may be a waymark on the rock ahead). After a little over 50m/yds, when the track peters out, take a path going up to the left (trousers or long socks will come in handy now). Beyond a STOCK CONTROL GATE the path turns left at the end of a WALLED VINEYARD. As the fencing curves round the end of the vineyard, the path forks: go right (❸). Look left for a large CAIRN here, by some kermes oaks.

Very shortly cross over a DRIED-UP WATERCOURSE with collapsed sides. The route is very sparsely waymarked with CAIRNS, but keep it in mind that you want to climb onto and over the ridge ahead. At this point it's also worth noting a square-cornered gap ahead, high in the mountainside — that's where you're going!

When you join a track (**50min**), *take note of the spot* (❹) so that you can pick up the path again on your return. Turn left on the track and make your way through a GATE. (If you meet a fence before the track, walk right

On the ascent and descent from Tripiti, your views encompass Mount Samitos and a reservoir in the Ligiotis Valley.

Áno Méros

Kaloidena

Plateau

Tripiti

0   1 km
0.5 mi

to find the track, then go through the gate.) There is a CAIRN on the far side of the track opposite where you came up to it, indicating your ongoing path. When you next meet track (**1h**) turn right and keep heading uphill. There *are* paths short-cutting loops off this track, but you may find yourselves following goat-paths to nowhere; on the ascent it is easier to keep to the track. Use the short-cuts to descend, when you can see where you are heading. Soon the 'square-cornered' gap in the ridge ahead can be clearly seen.

In **1h50min** you reach the TOP OF THE RIDGE. Up to the left is a smelly CAVE/STOCKADE! The track soon ends at a grey WATER

STORAGE TANK (**5**) on the right. If a mist has descended it is *not* advisable to climb beyond this point because there is no waymarking. Hopefully conditions will allow you to press on to a more inviting goal. When you are abreast of the storage tank, turn left uphill and walk to the right of the stone outcrop in front of you, towards a LONE KERMES OAK (**6**). Walk to the right of that tree with its holly-like leaves, and down across a small PLATEAU/GRAZING AREA (there are some large cairns). From here you can see a small concrete trig point marking the Tripiti viewpoint. Make your own way, scrambling up to it where you feel is easiest. Approaching from the left is probably best. There is a cairn at the top on the left, and the **Tripiti** TRIG POINT is to the right (**7**; **2h10min**). This is a tremendous viewpoint; it feels miles from anywhere. You look out over the Mesara Plain — where Festos and Agia Triada are sited — and across to the little island of Paximadia, just off the coast. The peninsula that juts out into the sea from Agia Galini is also visible in the distance.

Retrace your steps from here, taking advantage of some of the short-cut paths. You should be back at the CHURCH (**○**) in **Ano Meros** in **4h**.

Walk 29: CIRCUIT FROM MIXOROUMA VIA FRATI

Distance: 13.4km/8.3mi; 3h55min

Grade: ● moderate; straight-forward ascent/descent of 610m/2000ft on good shepherds' 4X4 tracks. The ascent is divided into two main sections, one at the start, the second about halfway through the walk.

Equipment: walking trainers or boots, sunhat, picnic, water

Picnic: Megalopotamos River

Access: 🚌 to/from Rethimnon (Timetable 1); journey time 1h. Then 🚌 to/from Mixorouma (Timetable 20); journey time about 45min. Or 🚗 to/from Mixorouma (35° 13.146'N, 24° 30.448'E).

T his is a lovely walk in a well cultivated valley with spectacular views of the high hills and crags around the Kourtaliotiko Gorge. In spring, there are wildflowers galore. Some frescoed Byzantine churches lie along your route, and there is the opportunity to stop almost exactly halfway round — at the village of Frati, where there is both a taverna and a *cafeneion*.

The bus stops in the village of **Mixorouma** along the main road heading south to Spili. **To start the walk (O)**, continue walking east towards Spili, until you reach a sign denoting the eastern end of the village. Just alongside the last building in the village turn right on an asphalt road signposted to the village of 'MOURNE'. As the road heads steeply downhill towards the river, ignore any right or left turns for the moment. After you cross the river on a BRIDGE **(5min)**, your road begins to climb. Look out for the RUINED MILL on the left set among citrus trees. Continue on the road, climbing quite steeply, with several sharp bends.

About 10 minutes after the bridge **(15min)**, you will have rounded a left-hand bend and will see a small farm building ahead on the left. Just before you reach this building, take a concrete track heading right, uphill (it soon becomes a dirt and stone track). Ignore any minor tracks left and right and

just head uphill on what is obviously the main track. You will pass through two STOCK CONTROL GATES, the second just by a house near the top of the hill; please leave them as you find them.

Shortly after the house, you rejoin the asphalt road **(25min)**. Turn right into the village of **Mourne**. At the junction with the TRIG POINT on a crag above and ahead of you, take the wider road round to the left **(❷; 30min)** and go left at another junction almost immediately. About four minutes later, turn right at the T-junction. Turn right again at the next junction some 100m/yds further on. Make a third right turn after another 100m/yds, heading uphill and out of the village. (Some 30m/yds to your left at this point is a spring/washing area signposted 'TRADITIONAL FOUNT'). Then you come to the CEMETERY church of **Agios Georgios (45min)**, which has some stunning 14th-century frescoes inside.

125

Leaving Agios Georgios, turn right and continue steeply uphill on a minor asphalt road that soon becomes a concrete track … and then a dirt track. Follow this towards the top of the ridge. Ten minutes after leaving the church, turn right on the asphalt road (**55min**). After a short time, the views open out. At the highest point on this road, you reach a crossroads with a sign pointing left 'To Coast' (**❸**); *ignore* this and continue ahead. But just 30m/yds further on, the (now dirt) track splits three ways: take the track on the left (**1h10min**). Follow this for 15 minutes, to a crossroads (**1h25min**). Your ongoing route is downhill to the right, but first walk forward about 100m/yds to explore the next church — another **Agios Georgios** with more frescoes.

Returning to the start of your diversion, continue down the dirt track, ignoring minor turns left and right. After crossing a small WATERCOURSE (**1h35min**), turn left. Ignore a couple of tracks going off left, and your track will begin to climb again. Ten minutes after

the watercourse turn left at the T-junction by a small building with corrugated roof (**❹**; **1h45min**). The views to Frati and the Kourtaliotiko Gorge become quite spectacular along this section. Continue down the dirt track, which zigzags and becomes very steep. Shortly after one left-hand bend heavily reinforced with concrete and with rain gullies, the main track swings right and flattens out. At this point, ignore the track heading left downhill into the heart of a large olive grove. Soon you reach the bottom of the valley at a CONCRETE BRIDGE over the river **Megalopotamos** (**❺**; **2h**) — a pleasant picnic spot. From here the track winds uphill for about 25 minutes, into the village of **Frati** (**2h25min**), where you could take a break at the taverna or *cafeneion*.

Turn right on the asphalt road past some rental apartments and when you reach the CEMETERY CHURCH two minutes later, turn left on a minor asphalt road. This road soon becomes a dirt track and contours around a hillside high above the road leading into **Kourtaliotiko**

View to Frati (above) and frescoes in Agios Georgios church (left)

Gorge. Continue for some distance on this track, ignoring all side turnings. Eventually you will pass between TWO CHURCHES (**6**; **3h10min**), one to the left of the track and the other on the right, in an olive grove. Twenty minutes later, the E4 SIGN joins from the left, and there is a waymarking sign on an olive tree on your left

(**3h30min**). Continue ahead. Five minutes later, pass another CHURCH on your right; head right, uphill, here. The track becomes concrete and then asphalt as you enter the village of **Agia Pelagia**.

As the road from Frati joins yours from the right, continue ahead through the village. About 20m/yds past the last house, take the concrete track heading right and slightly uphill by the E4 MARKER POLE (**7**; **3h45min**). Pass a FARM BUILDING on your right (with a wind pump on the roof), and bear left when you meet another track. The village of Mixorouma is now visible to your left. At the end of the track, there is a wide open space with a spring ahead of you. Take the road heading 90° left, which meets the main road through **Mixorouma** in the centre of the village, near the BUS STOP (**○**; **3h55min**).

Walk 30: THE KAMARES CAVE

Distance: 10km/6.2mi; 6h
Grade: ● a very strenuous climb and descent of 1050m/3450ft; you must be sure-footed and agile. E4 waymarking poles interspersed with cairns; plenty of water en route
Equipment: walking trainers, sunhat, torch, picnic, water container, walking pole/s
Picnic: anywhere en route; there is ample shade
Access: 🚌 to/from Kamares (35° 9.182'N, 24° 49.176'E). There is also a 🚐 from Rethimnon on Mondays-Fridays (Timetable 19), but timings are too tight to complete the walk.

This is somewhat of an aerobic exercise to a huge cave where the original cache of elaborate Minoan pottery known as Kamares Ware was found; it is now on display in the museum in Iraklion. The splendid cave, with a mouth 42m wide and 19m high (135ft x 62ft), is large and explorable. If you go to the back, and left of centre, search carefully and you will find the opening down on the floor, about 5m/15ft wide, where the pottery was found, in a fissure. For experienced climbers and walkers with the appropriate gear, Kamares is a good starting/finishing point for expeditions to the Nidha Plateau and Psiloritis.

Leave your car down off the main road, outside the CHURCH (◎) in **Kamares**. **Start out** by heading east through the village. There's one of several pleasant old *cafeneions* just along on the left from the church. At the first fork, where there is a telegraph pole in the middle, keep straight on uphill (ignore Odos Ay Georgiou going off to the right). Within a few moments, at a three-way junction, fork left up 25TH MARCH STREET.

At the top of the hill you meet the main road. Cross straight over, onto an old concreted road. There are 'KAMARES' signs and maps on the wall at the left — as well as a handwritten sign in German saying 'Only on Foot' ('Nur zu Fuss') in a nice bit of understatement. After a five-minute pull uphill the concrete ends, and rough track continues. Look up to the right and notice the first E4 signpost. The path starts just beyond it, turning

hard back off the track; be sure to turn right here (don't go ahead towards the water tank). Remember to re-secure any stock control gates. The path turns steeply uphill, and the next E4 mark is on a tree. Keep your eye out for CAIRNS in the absence of E4 waymarking. Soon after the tree the path turns left and a WATER PIPE IN A CONCRETE CHANNEL (❶) starts on the right. This conduit accompanies you most of the way uphill, and several water troughs provide cold drinking water.

The path meets a track at a T-junction (**15min**; stock control gate); walk to the left and pick up the path again going up to the right, at the end of some ANIMAL DRINKING WELLS. The path turns right and forks (❷) just after an E4 waymark; crossing the hillside, look for CAIRNS to be sure of the route. As the path approaches the edge of a ravine, you have a fantastic view. From the viewpoint head back the way you've come and in three minutes you will be at a TROUGH where fresh water pours in off the mountainside.

In **1h30min**, as you climb into a band of trees, more CAIRN WAYMARKING starts. Ten minutes later, look left for a place to cut through the trees — mostly cypress and oak — and climb up onto a rock for a very good view into the Voulo ravine. The route flattens out, offering more views into the ravine. But before long the path is back in the trees and beginning to climb again. At **2h10min** there is another open TROUGH (**3**), with a noisy SLUICE. Continue beside the water conduit. The next open water TROUGH (**4**) with fresh water is ten minutes further up. The way forks here in front of the trough; go right (east), *always following the water conduit.*

Now the way is very steep and rough; you need to be sure-footed. Having swung round from the east and continued uphill — still guided by E4 signs — you will come to another

At the mouth of the enormous cave

WATER TROUGH. Five minutes later, having struggled up to a CONCRETE CISTERN (**5**), the path continues up to the right — across the front of the cistern. Fifteen minutes later the waymarks take you scrambling almost vertically up rocks. Five minutes later you will see the lip of the cave above, to the right of the path. At a BOULDER MARKED WITH FADED RED ARROWS, the path forks (**6**; **3h**). Head left, towards two lone kermes oaks. In **3h30min** you will be at the top, in the mouth of the **Kamares Cave** (**6**) — a pleasant place to relax before exploring.

Then retrace your steps to **Kamares** village (**O**; **6h**).

129

Walk 31: ELEFTHERNA

Distance: 7km/4.3mi; 1h45min (or up to 4h with diversions)
Grade: ● fairly easy ups and downs of about 150m/500ft, but some steep steps; a short part of the route is E4 waymarked
Equipment: walking trainers, sunhat, picnic, water, torch

Picnic: Byzantine tower or the Hellenistic bridge (1h-point)
Access: 🚐 to/from Rethimnon (Timetable 1); journey time 1h. Then 🚐 to/from Archaia Eleftherna (Timetable 18); journey 1h. Or 🚗 (35° 19.416'N, 24° 40.590'E).

This is a short walk in a lush green valley of olive, orange, cypress and pine trees — ablaze with wild flowers and cyclamen in spring. The spectacularly-sited Dorian city-state of Eleftherna (10th century BC) and a gem of a Hellenistic bridge are the main attractions. With the opening of a new museum and the necropolis in June 2016 (after an archaeological dig lasting some 30 years) there is far more to see than ever before. Unfortunately we went to press before we could recheck how much the site has changed in the last couple of years, but no doubt there will be many improvements. Do visit the museum either before or after your walk to make the most of the day.

Start out in the centre of the **Archaia Eleftherna (O)**: follow the road signposted to the ACROPOLIS TAVERNA and site for 200m/yds. An INTERPRE-TATION BOARD in the taverna car park shows you where you plan to walk and tells you about the ancient sites. Take the path immediately to the right of the taverna. In a minute you come to the BYZANTINE TOWER shown opposite; it rises on a north-pointing ridge between two streams, with steep drops on either side — an ideal defensive position for the ancient acropolis. This walk will take you to the bottom of the western valley (on your left as you face the tower), then north beyond where the two valleys meet, and back up the spine of the ridge.

Follow the ancient cobblestone path to the left of the tower — a good first picnic spot — and then go straight ahead for a few

130

minutes, before making a sharp left turn downhill (**①**). (To the right, the smaller path continuing to the north is the one you'll be returning on at the end of the walk.) Immediately on your left, as you round the bend, you'll see a row of ancient ROCK-CUT CISTERNS supported by massive stone columns; they are thought to be Roman or pre-Roman.

The path continues downhill, passing a limestone cliff on the left and a (dry) spring with water troughs. A minute later you come to a T-junction, where a track goes off to the left. Here take the earthen trail to the right; it curves left and, in one minute, you reach another T-junction. Go right (north) on the path with the black-and-yellow (E4) waymark. About three to four minutes along this path, turn left down some earthen steps to an E4 MARKER POLE. At the E4 pole, turn left on the path with the rustic handrail that cuts through the olive grove. At the end of this path, cross the stream bed and turn right immediately, to follow the course of the stream (E4 MARKER on a tree). About 30m/yds further on, head half-left on steps leading up the bank. You emerge on a narrow fenced-in path, with an olive grove on your left and pines on your right. At the end of this short path, next to an E4 MARKER POLE, turn half-left up the next set of steps. When you meet a road (**②**; **30min**), *don't* continue up the steps with the E4 way-marks; turn right on the road. In a few minutes, at the first hairpin bend to the right, you can see the new MUSEUM and ancient NECROPOLIS (**③**) across the valley (it's just 15 minutes there and back, but you may end up spending the day…).

From the bend, head north on a track. This track hairpins twice as it descends to the stream bed, eventually crossing it over a small concrete WATER DUCT (a small wall on the right). About 25 paces on from here, look out for an ANCIENT STEPPED PATH (**④**) climbing off to the right — your return route up the central ridge. For the moment, stay on the track which crosses ANOTHER CONCRETE DUCT, gradually

rising. When the track bends sharp right, take the path dipping down to the left at the apex of this first bend (open and re-close the wire fence). This steep and narrow path clings to a ledge on the eastern side of the valley, before descending to the stream bed. (Another fork in the path, a bit further on, also leads to the stream bed: in spring, if the stream is too full of water, keep to this upper path.) By either route, you will come to a HELLENISTIC BRIDGE (**⑤**; **1h**), one of the highlights of this walk and an ideal spot for a shady rest — and another lovely setting for a picnic.

Just beyond the chapel on the east side of the bridge, take the right-hand, uphill fork, until you emerge on an old, pleasantly overgrown track. (Unless it's blocked off, you could take another lovely diversion here, by turning left and following the track to where the valley opens out, and then returning to this point; see the map and allow 1h30min return.) The main walk turns *right* here, back towards the ridge of Archaia Eleftherna. You pass through a wire gate almost immediately, then join another track — the one you left earlier. Two sharp bends later you're back at the point where you took the path to the bridge.

Eleftherna's Byzantine tower

steps and flatter ground (from where you have good views over the valley). After about ten steep steps look for a red waymark on your left as the path flattens out. Bear right at a large olive tree (also with a red waymark), ignoring the faint track going left uphill. Soon this flatter path begins to rise and become stepped.

When the path splits at some rustic wooden railings, take the uphill path to the left. (The downhill path to the right leads back to the NECROPOLIS.) From here it's just five minutes to the top (ignore a faint track heading right, downhill).

At the top you reach a small plateau (**1h30min**). The path keeps to the western edge of the ridge, but archaeological buffs may wish to explore the fenced acropolis excavation site ahead.*
The main walk continues on the path for another 10 minutes or so, until you come back to the ANCIENT CISTERNS (**❶**). From here retrace your steps up the cobbled path, past the Byzantine tower and back to **Archaía Eléftherna (O; 1h45min**).

Retrace your steps to the ANCIENT STEPPED PATH (**❹**) mentioned earlier (now on your left) and take it. After a minute the path turns right up some crude steps. It winds up the hillside, alternating between crude

---

*To explore the ancient site, continue on the path following the western edge of the ridge. In four minutes take a small path climbing sharp left through a makeshift wire gate. There is a small ARCHAEOLOGICAL DIG on this plateau. Four minutes later, another sharp left turn leads to the next plateau, in the centre of which is the barrel-vaulted (roofless) church of **Agía Iríni**. Returning to the main path, a couple of minutes further on you come to the last of the little surprises: another path climbs a bank on the left up to another

plateau (only about 30m/yds wide). Cross to the far (eastern) side of it, to where you will find a path leading down to a 'ledge'. A few paces further on you will come to the entrance of an ANCIENT TUNNEL cut out of the rock. (A torch would come in handy here.) The entrance looks quite small, but the tunnel is surprisingly large once you are inside it. It was apparently used in ancient times to carry water from the cisterns to the dwellings on the eastern slope of the ridge.

BUS TIMETABLES

Bus times are *not* written in stone; seasonal changes are made in mid-May and mid-September. The timetables below represent the basic *summer* service. Extra buses run during the tourist season (May-October) for popular routes; buses are likely to be less frequent in spring and autumn. You can check www.e-ktel.com/en, but it's wise to collect an up-to-date timetable from the bus station. Enquire about early-morning buses in particular if you think there is one (ie, if we have stated that there is one) because there's a chance they'll think you wouldn't dream of getting up at the crack of dawn when you're on holiday! Note, too, that there are other buses running from the resorts: ask for local timetables when you arrive. **Express buses** are unlikely to stop at intermediate destinations. See Index to locate quickly the timetable number for each destination; see pages 8-9 for bus stations.

BUSES FROM HANIA

1 Hania-Rethimnon; daily; journey 1h (continues to Iraklion; see Timetable 2 below)
Departures from Hania: 05.30, 06.30, 07.30, 08.30, 09.30, 10.30, 11.30, 12.00 (via the old road), 12.30, 13.30, 14.30, 15.30, 16.30, 17.30, 18.30, 19.30, 20.30.
Express: 08.45, 09.15, 11.15
Departures from Rethimnon: 07.00, 07.30 (via the old road), 09.00, 10.00, 11.00, 12.00, 13.00, 14.00, 15.00, 16.00, 17.00, 18.00, 19.00, 20.00, 21.00, 22.00.
Express: 12.45, 13.45, 15.45

2 Hania-Iraklion (via Rethimnon); daily; journey 2h
Departures from Hania: as Timetable 1 above
Departures from Iraklion: 05.30, 06.30, 07.30, 08.30, 09.30, 10.30, 11.30, 12.00 (via the old road), 12.30, 13.30, 14.30, 15.30, 16.30, 17.30, 18.30, 19.30, 20.30.
Express: 11.15, 12.15, 14.15

3 Hania-Omalos; daily; journey about 45min
Departures from Hania: 06.15, 07.45, 08.45
Departures from Omalos: 07.30, 09.00, 13.30, 19.30

4 Hania-Hora Sfakion; daily; journey about 1h40min
Departures from Hania: 06.45, 08.15, 08.30, 11.00, 14.00, 16.00
Departures from Hora Sfakion: 07.00, 11.00, 13.30, 18.300

5 Hania-Paleohora; daily; journey 2h
Departures from Hania: 05.15, 08.45, 10.45, 12.45, 16.00, 20.00
Departures from Paleohora: 07.15, 12.00, 15.30, 18.15, 22.00

6 Hania-Sougia; daily; journey 1h45min
Departures from Hania: 05.00, 07.30 (Sundays only), 08.45, 13.45, 16.00
Departures from Sougia: 07.00 (Sundays only), 12.30, 18.30

7 Hania-Kolimbari; daily; journey 40min
Departures from Hania: 06.30, 07.15, 07.30, 08.00, 08.30, 09.00, 09.30, 10.00, 11.00, 11.30, 12.00, 12.30, 13.00, 13.15, 13.30, 14.00, 14.30, 15.00, 15.30, 16.30, 17.30, 18.00, 18.30, 19.30, 20.30, 21.00, 21.30, 22.00, 22.30, 23.00
Departures from Kolimbari: 05.15, 06.15, 07.15, 07.30, 08.00, 08.30, 09.00, 09.30, 10.00, 10.25, 11.10, 11.00, 11.30, 12.00, 12.30, 13.00, 13.30, 14.00, 14.10, 14.30, 15.00, 15.30, 16.00, 16.10, 17.10, 18.40, 18.50, 19.30, 20.30, 21.15, 21.40, 22.05

8 Hania-Kastelli-Kissamos; daily; journey 1h25min
Departures from Hania: 06.30, 07.15 (not Sat, Sun), 07.30 (only Sat, Sun), 08.30, 10.00, 11.00, 12.00, 13.00, 13.30 (only Sat, Sun), 14.30, 15.30, 16.30 (not Sat, Sun), 17.30, 18.30, 19.30, 20.30

133

Departures from Kastelli-Kissamos: 06.00, 07.00, 07.30 (not Sat, Sun), 08.00, 08.30, 09.30, 10.30, 11.30, 12.30, 14.00, 15.30, 16.30, 17.30, 18.30, 19.15

9 Hania–Kato Stalos–Agia Marina–Platanias–Maleme; daily
Departures from Hania: 06.30, 07.15, 08.00, 08.45 and every 15min until 11.00; 11.00 and every 30min until 23.00
Departures from Maleme Beach Hotel: 06.30, 07.15, 07.35, 07.55, 08.20, 08.45, 09.00 and every 15min until 11.15; 11.30 and every 30min until 22.00

10 Hania–Elafonisi (and Moni Chrisoskalitisas); daily; journey 1h15min
Departures from Hania: 09.00; *Departures from Elafonisi:* 16.00

BUSES FROM RETHIMNON

11 Rethimnon–Plakias; daily; journey 40min
Departures from Rethimnon: 05.30 (Mon-Fri *only*), 09.00, 11.00, 14.30, 18.00
Departures from Plakias: 07.00 (Mon-Fri *only*), 10.00, 12.00, 15.15, 19.00

12 Rethimnon–Hania; daily; journey 1h
Departures from Rethimnon; Departures from Hania: See Timetable 1

13 Rethimnon–Iraklion; daily; journey 1h30min
Departures from Rethimnon: 06.30, 07.30 (via the old road), 07.45, 08.30, 08.45, 09.15, 09.45, 10.15, 10.45, 11.15, 11.45, 12.15, 12.45, 13.15, 13.45, 14.00, 14.15, 14.45, 15.15, 15.45, 16.15, 16.45, 17.15, 17.45, 18.15, 18.45, 19.45, 20.45, 21.45. *Express: 09.45, 10.15, 12.15*
Departures from Iraklion: See Timetable 2

14 Rethimnon–Preveli; daily; journey 40min
Departures from Rethimnon: 09.00, 11.00, 14.30
Departures from Preveli: 11.30, 14.30, 18.30

15 Rethimnon–Asomatos–Plakias; daily; journey 40min
Departures from Rethimnon: 06.15 (not Sat, Sun), 10.00, 14.15, 16.30
Departures from Plakias: 07.00, 09.00 (only Sat, Sun), 11.45, 15.00, 18.00

16 Rethimnon–Hora Sfakion; daily; journey 1h30min
Departures from Rethimnon: 08.00, 14.15 (not Sat, Sun)
Departures from Hora Sfakion: 11.00 (not Sat, Sun), 17.30, 19.00

17 Rethimnon–Omalos; daily; journey 2h30min
Departures from Rethimnon: 06.15, 07.00
Departures from Omalos: via Hania; see Timetable 3 above

18 Rethimnon–Eleftherna; daily; journey 1h
Departures from Rethimnon: 06.15, 10.30, 12.45
Departures from Eleftherna: 07.00, 11.05, 16.00

19 Rethimnon–Timbaki–Mires (for Kamares); Mon-Fri; journey 1h30min-2h
Departure from Rethimnon: 07.00; *Departure from Kamares:* 13.50

20 Rethimnon–Mixorouma–Spili–Agia Galini; daily; journey 1h30
Departure from Rethimnon: 07.00, 10.30, 14.15
Departure from Mixorouma: 10.00, 12.30, 14.30, 16.30 (Mon-Fri), 09.00, 12.30, 16.30 (Sat/Sun); *recheck departure times from Mixorouma in advance!*

BUSES FROM KASTELLI-KISSAMOS (see also Timetable 8 above)

21 Kastelli–Hania–Omalos; daily; journey 3h
Departures from Kastelli-Kissamos: 05.00, 06.00, 07.00, 14.00
Departures from Omalos: via Hania; see Timetable 3 above

22 Kastelli–Hania–Hora Sfakion; daily; journey 3h45min
Departures from Kastelli-Kissamos: via Hania; see Timetables 4 and 8
Departures from Hora Sfakion: 17.30

● *Index*

Geographical names comprise the only entries in this Index. For other entries, see Contents, page 3. A page number in *italic type* indicates a map reference; a page number in **bold type** indicates a photograph. Both of these may be in addition to a text reference on the same page. Bus timetables are on pages 133-134.

135